A Guide to CONSTELLATIONS

By Gib Goodfellow
and Liz Stenson

Series Literacy Consultant
Dr Ros Fisher

Pearson Education Limited
Edinburgh Gate
Harlow
Essex CM20 2JE
England

www.longman.co.uk

The rights of Gib Goodfellow and Liz Stenson to be identified as the authors of this Work have been asserted by them in accordance with the Copyright, Designs and Patents Act, 1988.

Text Copyright © 2004 Pearson Education Limited. Compilation Copyright © 2004 Dorling Kindersley Ltd. All rights reserved. No part of this publication may be reproduced, stored in a retrieval system or transmitted in any form or by any means electronic, mechanical, photocopying, recording, or otherwise, without either the prior written permission of the publishers and copyright owners or a licence permitting restricted copying in the United Kingdom issued by the Copyright Licensing Agency Ltd., 90 Tottenham Court Road, London W1P 9HE

ISBN 0 582 84151 8

Colour reproduction by Colourscan, Singapore
Printed and bound in China by Leo Paper Products Ltd.

The Publisher's policy is to use paper manufactured from sustainable forests.

10 9 8 7 6 5 4 3

The following people from **DK** have contributed to the development of this product:

Art Director Rachael Foster

Martin Wilson **Managing Art Editor**	**Managing Editor** Marie Greenwood
Peter Radcliffe **Design**	**Editorial** Steve Setford, Selina Wood
Brenda Clynch **Picture Research**	**Production** Gordana Simakovic
Richard Czapnik, Andy Smith **Cover Design**	**DTP** David McDonald

Consultant Carole Stott

Dorling Kindersley would like to thank: Alastair Muir and Chanele Dandridge; Rose Horridge, Hayley Smith and Gemma Woodward in the DK Picture Library; LizTyndall for editorial assistance; Johnny Pau for additional cover design work; Gavin Dunn for illustrations; Royal Greenwich Observatory.

Picture Credits: AKG London: Nimatallah 6r. Corbis: Bettmann 5cr. DK Images: British Museum 5bl. Galaxy Picture Library: Gordon Garradd 35cl; Y. Hirose 1; Michael Stecker 32tr. Science Photo Library: Luke Dodd 25tr; European Southern Observatory 19cr; Magrath Photography 4; NOAO 30c; Pekka Parviainen 7tr; John Sanford 14br; Eckhard Slawik 15cl; Space Telescope Science institute/NASA 7bl; Frank Zullo 3.
Jacket: Science Photo Library: Luke Dodd front t.

All other images: Dorling Kindersley © 2004. For further information see www.dkimages.com
Dorling Kindersley Ltd., 80 Strand, London WC2R ORL

Contents

What Is a Constellation?	4
Stargazing	5
Constellations of the Zodiac	11
Constellations of the Northern and Southern Celestial Spheres	20
Glossary	39
Constellations Index	40

What Is a Constellation?

Since ancient times, people have looked up at the night sky and observed the great number of stars. Ancient stargazers tried to make sense of the sky by picturing certain patterns of stars as creatures from **myths**. These star patterns were the first **constellations**. Later, **astronomers**, or scientists who study the universe, began to map the night sky. They gave names and shapes to the constellations.

A Guide to Constellations is full of information about constellations, including how they came to be named. Each entry shows a star map of the constellation and explains what kinds of stars and other **celestial** objects appear in it. The italic labels on the star map show the positions in the sky of nearby constellations. A world map indicates the best time of year for viewing and shows the degrees of latitude from where the constellation can best be seen. White bands on the world map indicate varying degrees of visibility. The whitest bands show where the constellation is least visible.

Today, astronomers use high-powered telescopes to study stars. This is the Keck Observatory on Mauna Kea in Hawaii.

Stargazing

Ancient astronomers noticed that the stars seemed to stay in the same position relative to each other but moved across the sky on regular schedules. They rose, set or disappeared altogether at predictable times during the night or in a season. It was as if Earth were in the centre of a huge, slowly turning sphere covered with pinpricks that let light shine through.

Because specific constellations appear to change their location or even disappear from view during some parts of the year, constellations were used to plan the year. For example, seeing a particular constellation in the sky might signal the time to plant crops. Constellations were also important to sailors and other travellers, who used them to guide their journeys.

The Greek astronomer Hipparchus (hip-PAR-kus) observed the stars more than 2,000 years ago. This picture wrongly shows him using an instrument called a cross-staff, which was not invented until much later.

This clay model from ancient Egypt shows a farmer plowing. The Egyptians and other ancient peoples used the constellations to plan the farming seasons.

Ancient Greek scholars named many of the **constellations** and used their **myths** to explain patterns they saw in the stars. Although the Greek names are the best known by Western societies, nearly every culture has its own names for the constellations they saw.

Some stars are visible only from the Northern or Southern hemispheres. In AD 150, the Greek scientist Ptolemy wrote a book that described forty-eight constellations. This book is the basis for our current knowledge of Northern Hemisphere constellations.

In 1603, the German astronomer Johann Bayer published a star atlas that included some of the constellations visible in the Southern Hemisphere. Then, in the 1750s, a French astronomer Nicolas Louis de Lacaille (lah-KAH-yuh) introduced fourteen more constellations seen from the Southern Hemisphere.

Atlas, a figure from Greek mythology, is depicted in this sculpture holding a globe showing many of the constellations known to the ancient Greeks. Some of them are labelled here.

Asterisms

Some constellations contain smaller groups of stars that also form patterns. These groups are called **asterisms**. The Big Dipper, or the Plough, for example, is a familiar asterism. It is part of a constellation called Ursa Major.

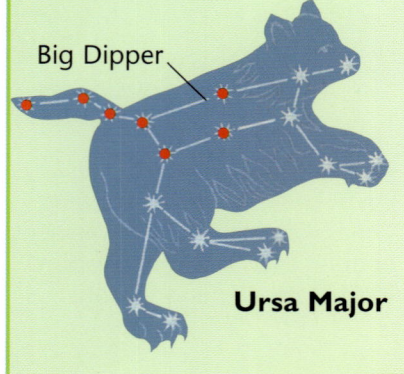

Stars and Other Celestial Bodies

On a clear night, thousands of points of light in the sky can be seen. These are stars, but other **celestial** objects, such as planets and comets, are sometimes visible as well. Stars are made of glowing gases that produce light and other energy. The stars appear to twinkle but actually do not. The twinkling is caused by air moving in Earth's atmosphere. Air distorts the starlight as it travels through the atmosphere, so the light appears to flicker, or twinkle.

Comets are balls of snow, ice, gas and dust that orbit the Sun.

Some stars appear to be brighter than others. Some really are brighter because they are producing more light. Others seem brighter to us because they are closer to Earth.

The Greek astronomer Hipparchus invented a system in which he rated the **magnitude**, or brightness, of a star from 1 to 6. The lower the number, the brighter the star is. In the 19th century, **astronomers** extended that system to include negative numbers for very bright stars. For example, the Sun, our closest star, is assigned a magnitude of about –26.7. The faintest stars seen with the naked eye have a magnitude of about 6.

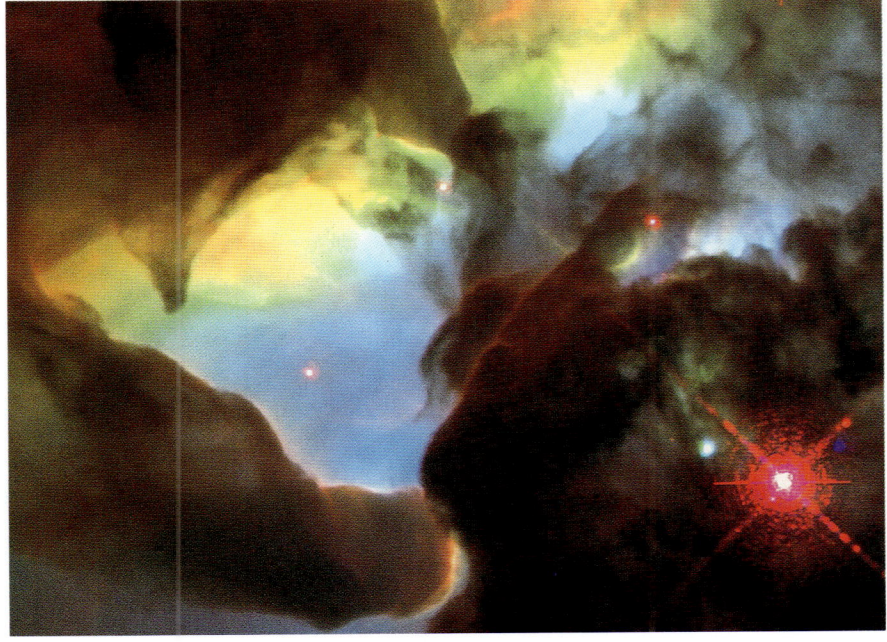

Stars are born in huge clouds of gas and dust in space. Such a cloud is called a **nebula**. This is part of the Lagoon Nebula in the constellation of Sagittarius.

Star Maps

Star maps make it possible to locate stars and other objects in the night sky. **Astronomers** use different kinds of star maps. One such map is the **celestial sphere**, a giant imaginary sphere with Earth at its centre. Astronomers have labelled it with a north celestial pole, a south celestial pole, an **equator** and imaginary lines similar to latitude and longitude on Earth. These coordinates help astronomers locate stars, **constellations** and **galaxies**.

Stars stay in the same place on the celestial sphere, but because of the Earth's rotation, they appear to move across the sky. As some appear on the eastern horizon, for example, others disappear over the western horizon.

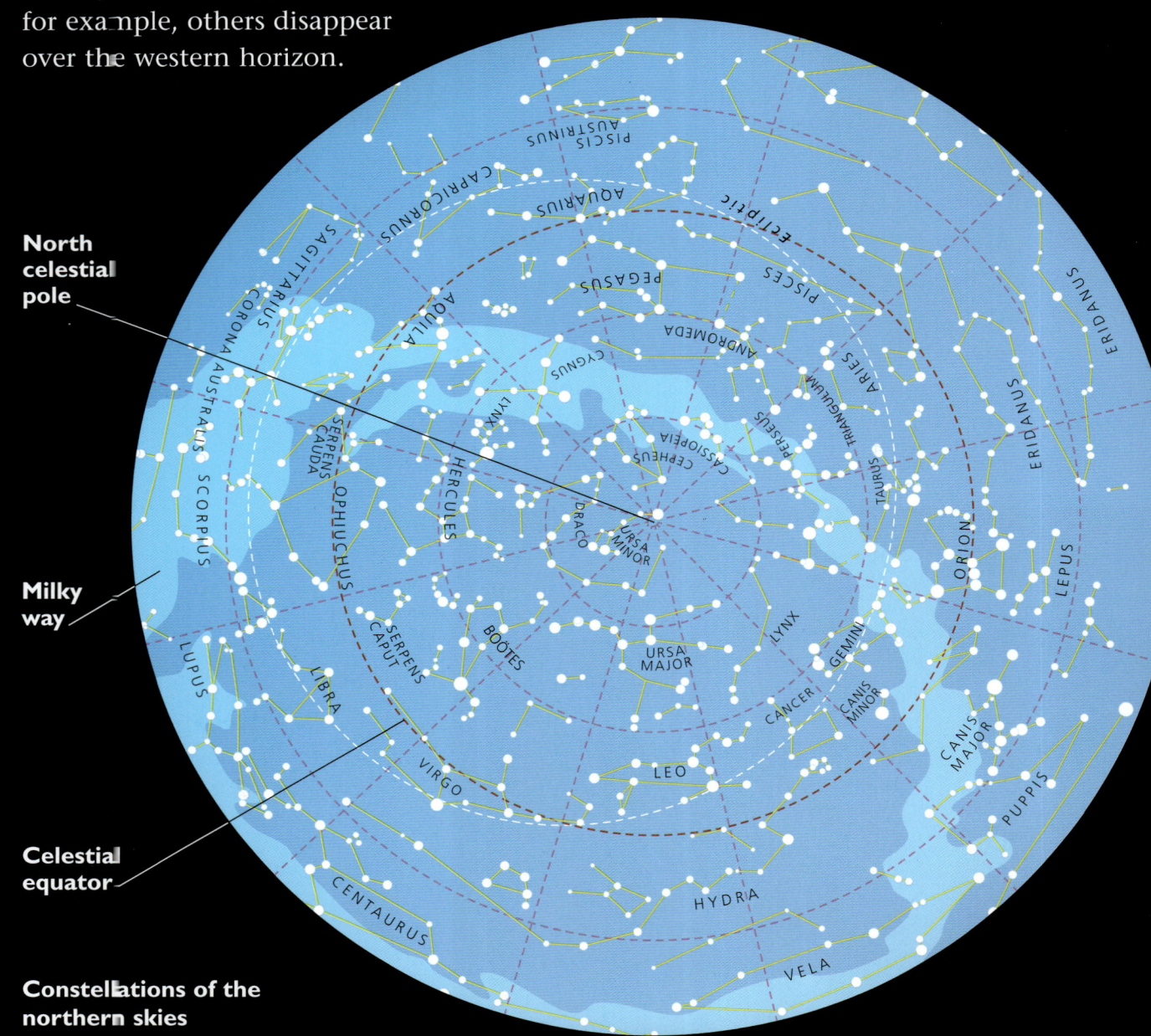

North celestial pole

Milky way

Celestial equator

Constellations of the northern skies

The stars that can be seen in one night depend on the location on Earth, the date and the time. In the Northern Hemisphere, stars in the northern half of the celestial sphere can be seen, whereas in the Southern Hemisphere, stars in the celestial sphere's southern half can be seen. Closer to the equator, more of the stars in the other hemisphere can be seen.

Flat sky maps or a tool called a **planisphere** or star wheel help people observe stars. Flat sky maps are made by dividing the image of the celestial sphere into sections, then flattening each section. (See page 10 for more about sky maps.) Turning the map of a planisphere shows which stars will be above for any given date or hour.

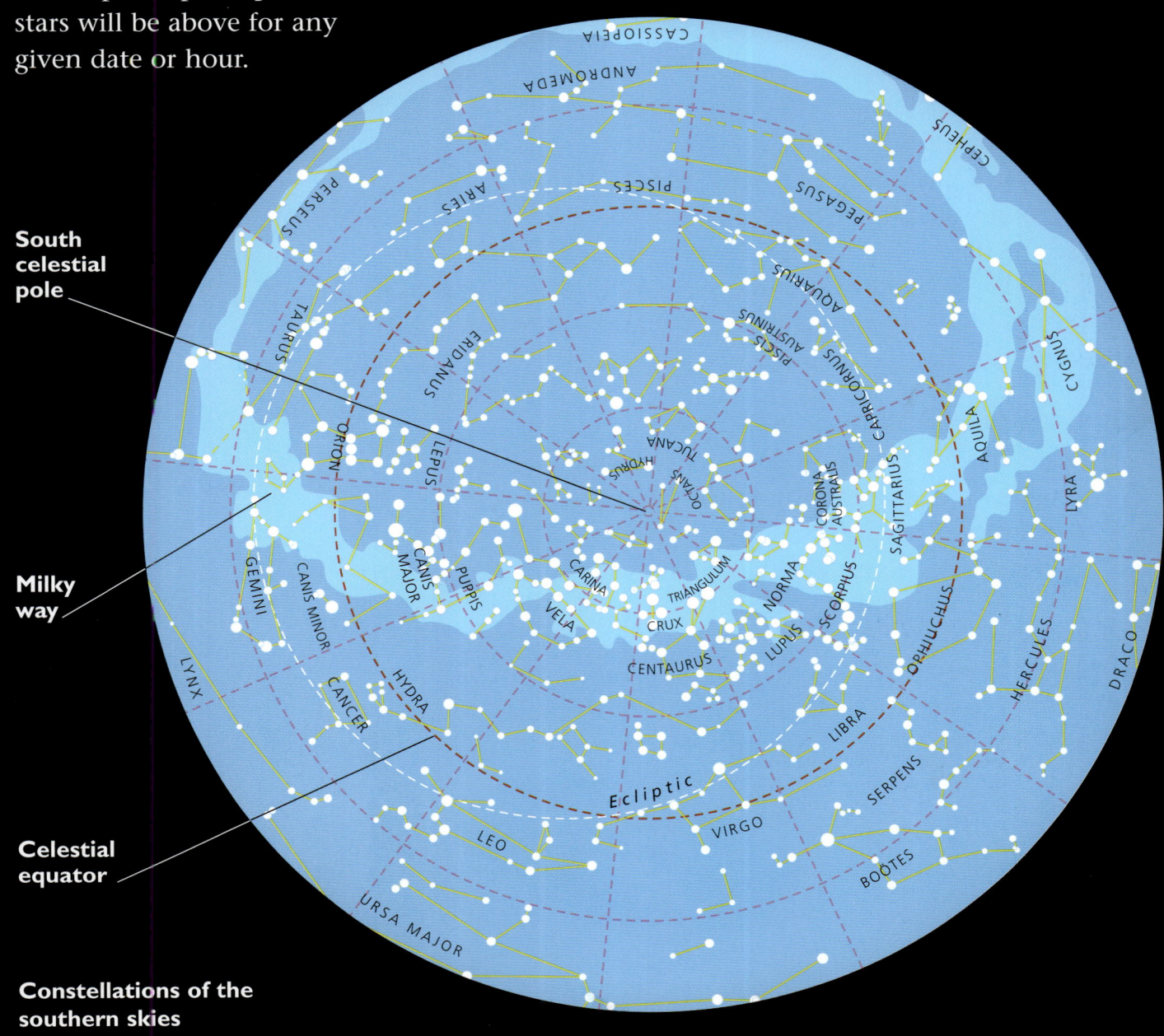

Constellations of the southern skies

Using a Sky Map or Planisphere

You can find sky maps for viewing stars in your hemisphere each month online at websites such as www.Skymaps.com. Astronomy magazines available at your local bookshop also have monthly sky charts, and you may find them printed in the newspapers as well. These maps will show you where in the sky to look for a constellation during a particular time of year. An example showing **constellations** visible at night in the Southern Hemisphere during September is to the right. First find north on a compass, then facing north, hold the map over your head so that the section labelled north points toward the northern sky. With north in front of you overhead, south is behind you, east is on your right, and west is on your left.

You can buy a planisphere at a bookstore. Turn the wheel so the date lines up with the time of night you will be stargazing. The stars in the centre oval will be visible at that time. To use the planisphere, find north and follow the instructions for the sky map.

This sky map shows constellations visible during September.

Other Helpful Stargazing Equipment

- A flashlight. If you cover the light with red cellophane, your night vision will be better.
- A compass
- An observation journal

Tips for Best Viewing

- Have an adult with you.
- It is best to be away from streetlights or the lights of buildings. A full Moon can limit viewing.

You can set your planisphere to show the stars visible at a specific time and location.

Constellations of the Zodiac

This chapter lists alphabetically the twelve constellations of the **zodiac**, which can be seen from both hemispheres. For an explanation of the format of each entry, see page 4.

The constellations of the zodiac are found along the **ecliptic**, the path the Sun follows each year. They were the first constellations to be identified and named. Today, we use their Greek names and stories, although many other ancient cultures made up stories and names for these same constellations.

The Ecliptic

Long ago people observed that the Sun, as it travels along the ecliptic, appears to pass in front of twelve constellations. These constellations, known as the zodiac, are almost equally spaced, so the Sun remains in each constellation for about a month.

In fact, the Sun also crosses a thirteenth constellation, Ophiuchus (the Serpent Bearer), which has not been recognized as a full member of the zodiac.

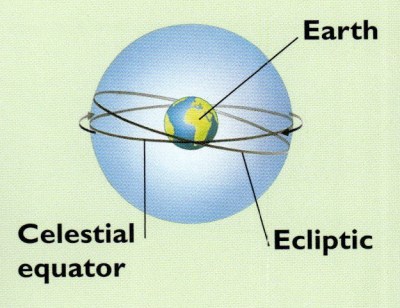

The Constellations of the Zodiac

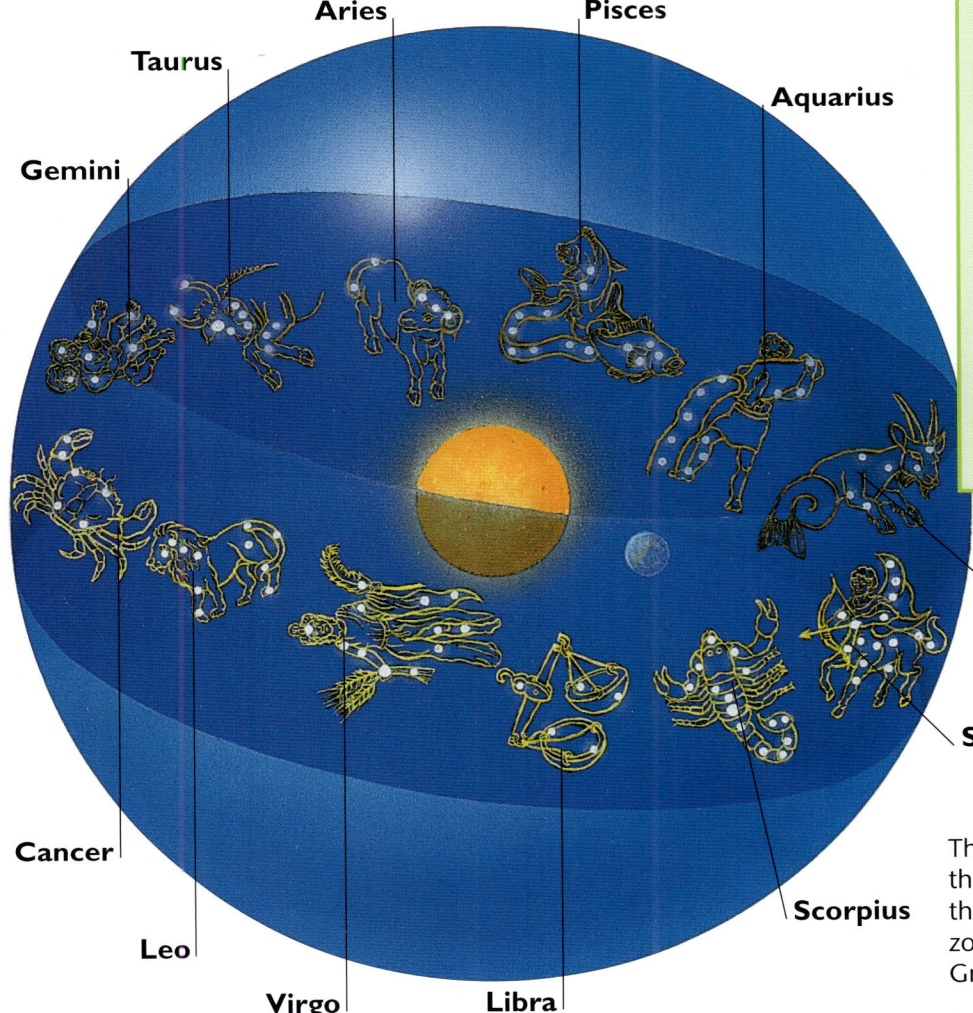

The constellations along the ecliptic – the path along which the Sun moves through the sky – are known as the zodiac, a name that comes from the Greek word for animals.

Aquarius

(ah-KWAHR-ee-uhs), the Water Carrier

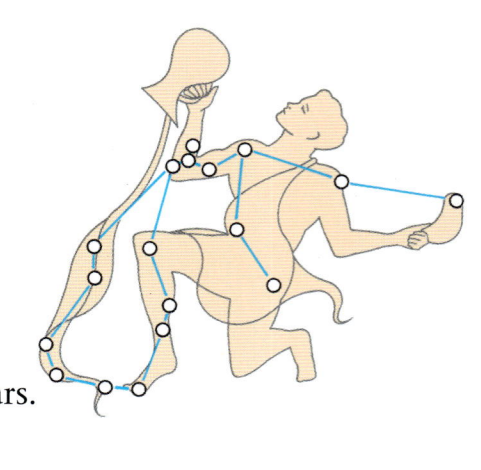

The stars of Aquarius are fainter than most others in the **zodiac constellations**. The brightest stars in Aquarius have **magnitudes** of around 3, and others have magnitudes of around 4. Most of the stars in Aquarius are visible with binoculars.

Aquarius, the water carrier, represents a prince of Troy. Troy was an ancient city in what is now Turkey. The prince was taken to live with the gods and serve them water. In this constellation, the prince pours water from a jar into the mouth of a large fish (not shown here; see page 33).

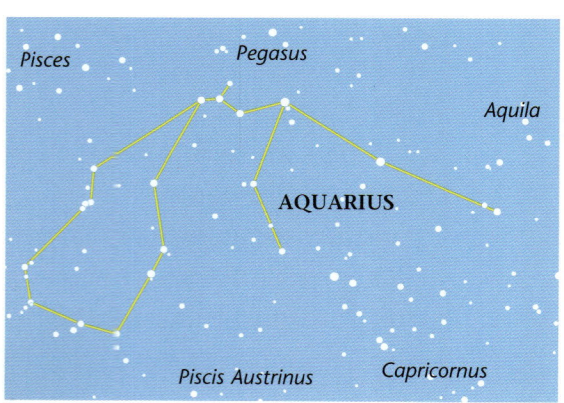

Best Viewing Time

August to October
Where: 65°N–86°S

Aries

(AIR-eez), the Ram

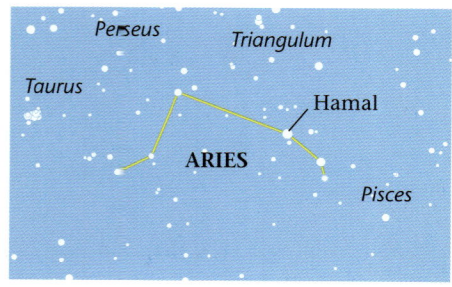

Aries is one of the smaller constellations of the zodiac. Its most noticeable feature is a line of three stars in the head of the ram, but it has only one bright star, Hamal. This name comes from Arab **astronomers**, who called the star Ras al Hamal, or Head of the Sheep.

Aries is considered by many to be the first sign in the zodiac. In ancient Greece, when the season of spring began, the Sun entered Aries. Today, Pisces is in that position.

Aries was a ram with a golden fleece, or hide. For more information about this important animal from Greek mythology, see page 34.

Best Viewing Time

November to December
Where: 90°N–58°S

Cancer

(CAN-sur), the Crab

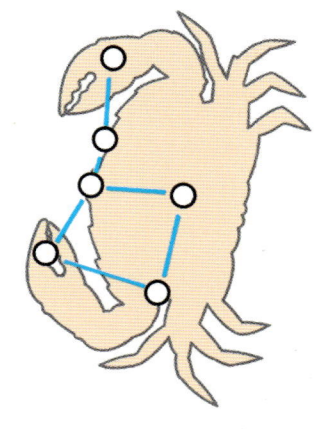

Cancer's brightest star is about magnitude 3.5. With binoculars, it is possible to see a cluster of stars within Cancer called the Beehive Cluster or Praesepe (the Manger). This field of stars appears to be more than three times wider than our full Moon. To find the Beehive Cluster, look halfway between Regulus in Leo and Pollux in Gemini.

In Greek mythology, Cancer was a giant crab. It was sent to distract the hero Hercules as he fought Hydra, a many-headed monster. The powerful Hercules managed to step on the crab and still kill Hydra.

Best Viewing Time

February to March
Where: 90°N–57°S

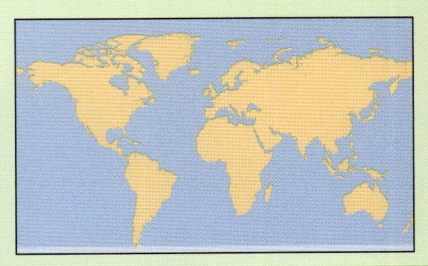

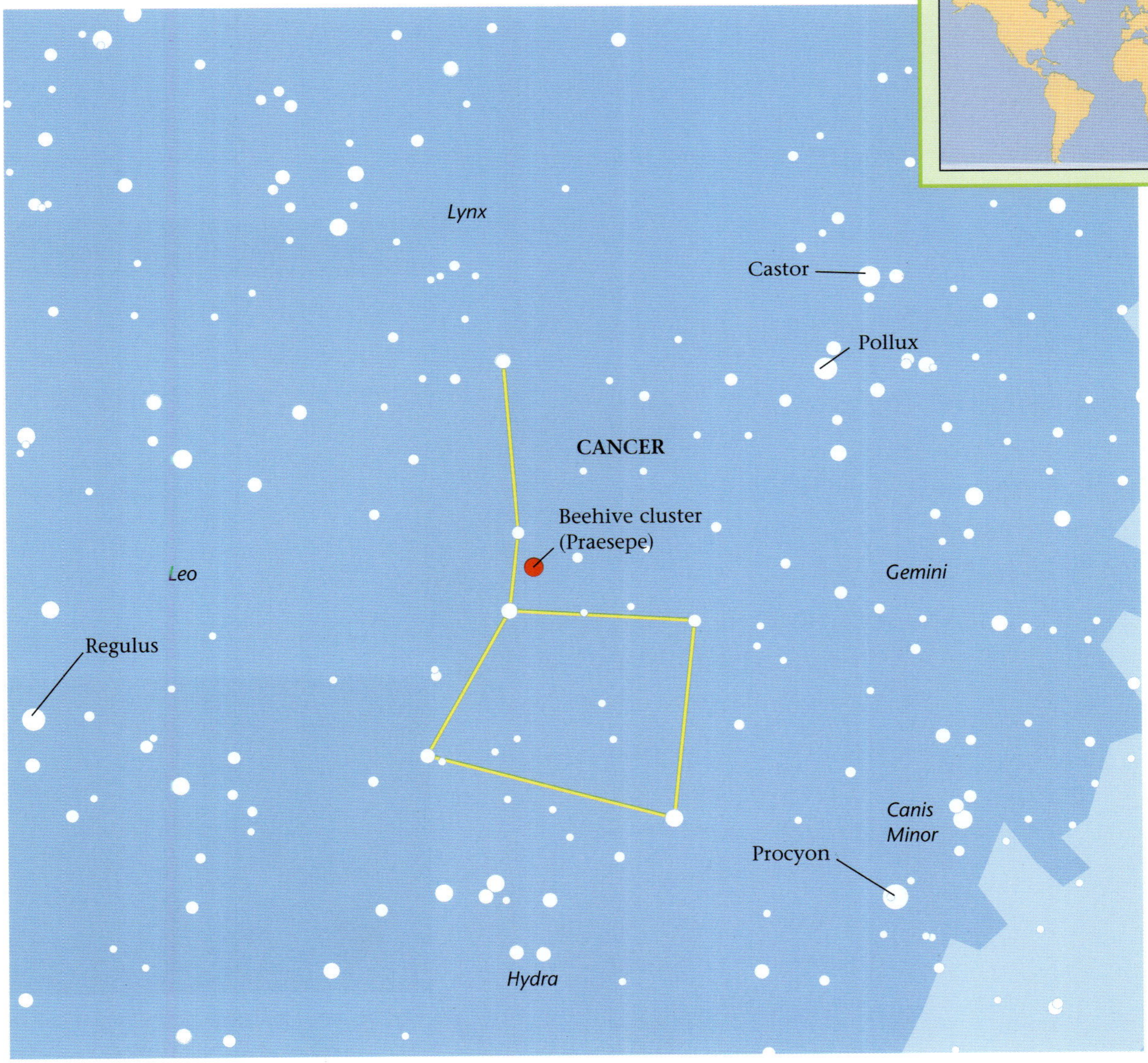

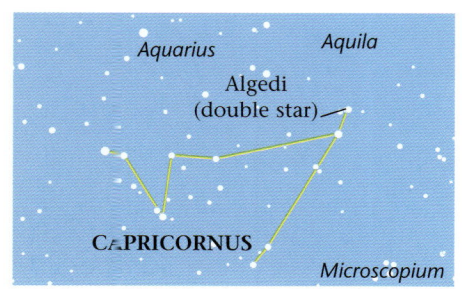

Capricornus

(CAP-ree-KOHR-nuhs),
the Sea Goat

Capricornus is the smallest constellation of the **zodiac**. It contains a **double star** known as Algedi. The **magnitudes** of the stars in Capricornus range from around 2.9 upward.

Capricornus is another mythical animal – a goat with a fish's tail. In Greek **myths**, the goat-like god Pan turned his lower half into a fish so he could escape from the sea monster Typhon.

Best Viewing Time

August to September
Where: 62°N–90°S

Gemini

(JEH-mih-ny), the Twins

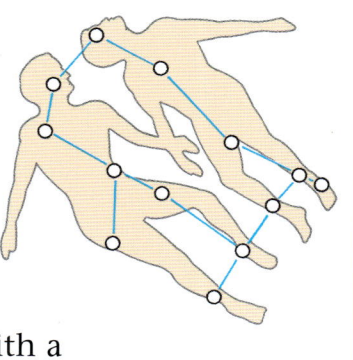

Gemini's two brightest stars, Castor and Pollux, are easily seen. Castor, with a magnitude of around 2, is actually a pair of bright stars. Pollux, with a magnitude of 1.14, is the brighter of the two.

Castor and Pollux were the twin sons of Queen Leda of Sparta. They went with Jason in his ship the *Argo* to find the Golden Fleece. Their task was to protect the crew, known as Argonauts. Some now regard the twins as mythical protectors of sailors. See page 34 for more information on the *Argo*.

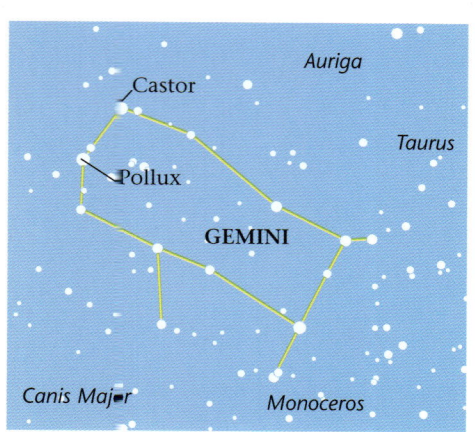

Best Viewing Time

January to February
Where: 90°N–55°S

These two bright stars are Pollux (bottom) and Castor (top).

Leo

(LEE-oh), the Lion

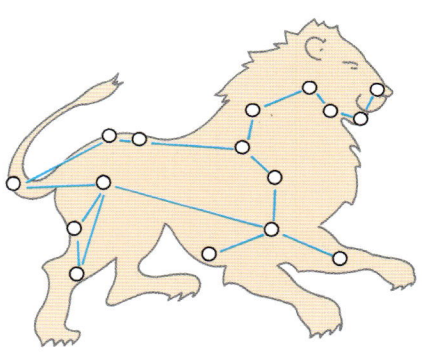

Leo is one of the easiest **constellations** to find because it has several stars of magnitude 3 or brighter. The brightest star, Regulus, is very close to the **ecliptic**. Leo's head and chest are formed by six stars arranged in a pattern that looks like a hook. These six stars form an **asterism** called the Sickle.

In Greek mythology, Leo was the lion killed by Hercules as the first of twelve labours Hercules was given to perform. Long before the Greeks created their myths, the Egyptians also saw this constellation as a lion. Its appearance in the sky each year coincided with the beginnings of summer, when the River Nile flooded and watered the crops. For this reason, the Egyptians worshipped the lion constellation.

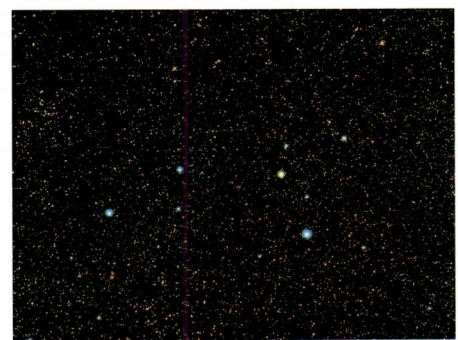

The main stars in Leo

Best Viewing Time

March to April
Where: 82°N–57°S

15

Libra

(LEE-brah), the Scales

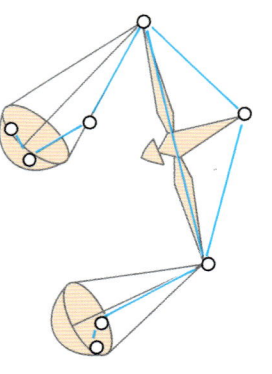

Libra is immediately west of Scorpius and just south of the **equator** on the **celestial sphere**. Libra used to be the claws of the constellation Scorpius. Its two brightest stars, with **magnitudes** of 2.8 and 2.6, have Arabic names that mean "southern claw" and "northern claw". The northern claw looks greenish. The other stars in the constellation are not easily visible.

More than 2,000 years ago, the Romans saw Libra as a balance scale. Now, Libra is usually drawn as scales held by the nearby figure of Virgo, the goddess of justice. Libra is the only non-living symbol in the Greek **zodiac**.

Best Viewing Time

May to June
Where: 60°N–90°S

Pisces

(PY-seez), the Fish

The brightest star in Pisces is a **double star** called Alresha, with a magnitude of 4. At one end of Pisces is an interesting **asterism** called the Circlet, formed from seven stars in a circle.

The constellation Pisces represents two fish. Their tails are tied with a cord, an image that first appeared in Babylonia and was passed on to Greece. In one Greek myth, the two fish represent Aphrodite, the goddess of love, and her son Eros, or Cupid. In the story, they jumped into a river to escape the sea monster Typhon.

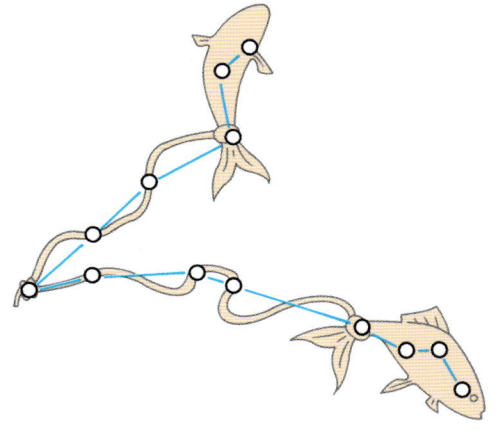

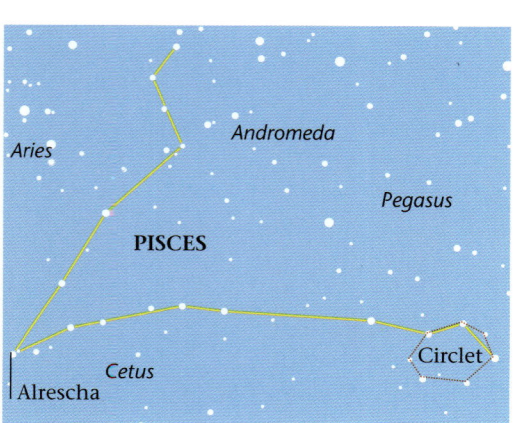

Best Viewing Time

October to November
Where: 83°N–56°S

Sagittarius

(sah-jit-TAIR-ee-uhs), the Archer

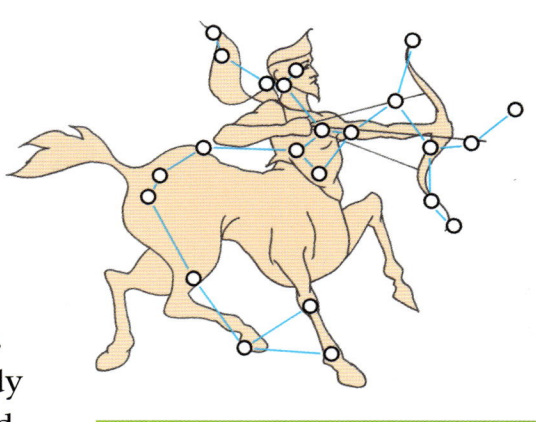

Sagittarius is located toward the centre of the **Milky Way** galaxy. In this area, groups of stars are much more dense, or tightly packed together. Sagittarius is a centaur, a creature with the chest and head of a man and the body and legs of a horse. Sagittarius's bow and arrow are traced by eight stars that form an **asterism** called the Teapot. This group looks like an outline of a teapot with a pointed lid and a large spout.

The figure was said to be the centaur Crotus, the son of the Greek god Pan and the inventor of archery. He is aiming his bow at a scorpion, represented by the neighbouring constellation of Scorpius. The Chinese saw this same constellation as a tiger. Ancient Arabs viewed it as ostriches drinking from the Milky Way.

Best Viewing Time

July to August
Where: 44°N–90°S

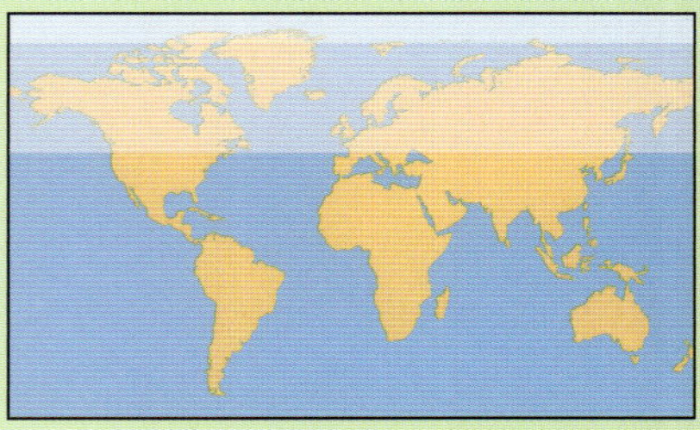

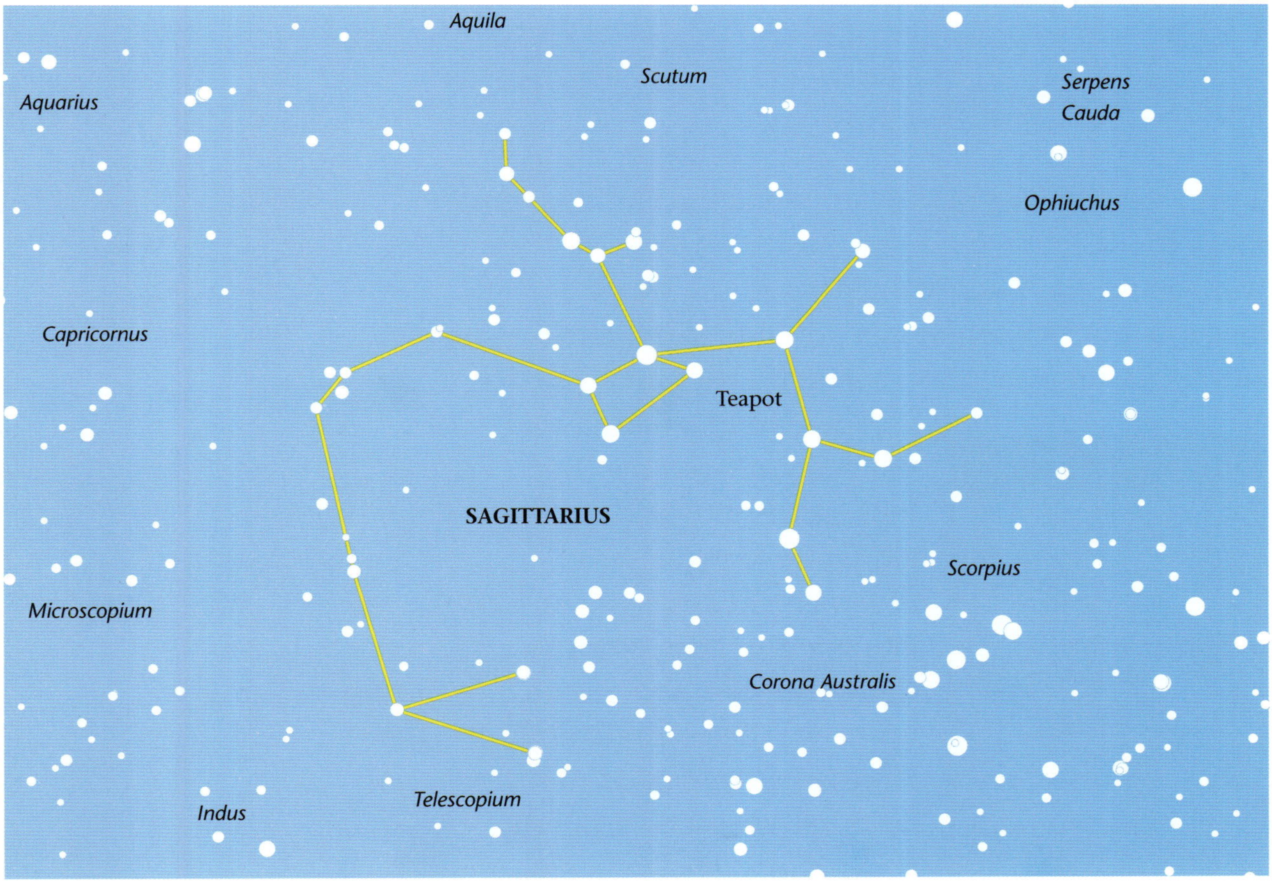

17

Scorpius

(SKOR-pee-uhs), the Scorpion

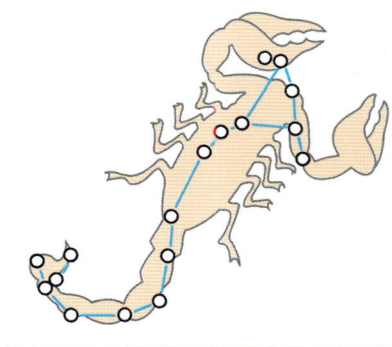

Scorpius, like Sagittarius, has the densely packed stars of the **Milky Way** in the background. Scorpius is easy to find. It looks like a scorpion, with its hooked tail. Antares, a star of about **magnitude** 1, is its heart. Shaula, a star of about magnitude 2, is in the stinger.

In Greek mythology, the hunter Orion, after killing many animals, bragged that no animal could kill him. The goddess of Earth, Gaia, was not pleased and sent Scorpius to silence him. The scorpion stung Orion to death.

Best Viewing Time

June to July
Where: 44°N–90°S

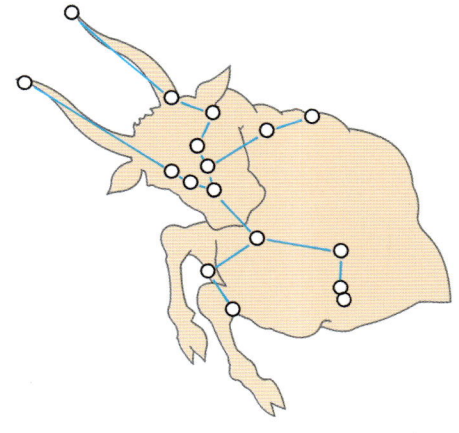

Taurus

(TAWR-uhs), the Bull

Many cultures have looked at stars and imagined a bull's head in the sky. The large star cluster Hyades (HY-uh-deez) marks the head of Taurus and the star Aldebaran is one eye. A well-known group of stars called the Pleiades (PLEE-uh-deez) is on the bull's back.

The Greeks believed that the god Zeus became the bull Taurus in order to kidnap Princess Europa of Phoenicia. After the kidnapping, Zeus swam to Crete with the princess on his back. The constellation represents the part of the bull that would be visible above the water.

Best Viewing Time

December to January
Where: 88°N–58°S

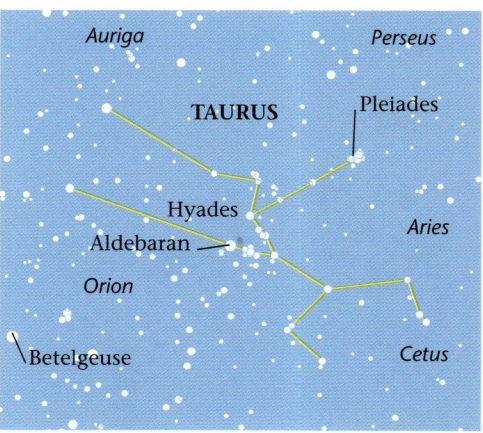

18

Virgo

(VER-goh), the Virgin

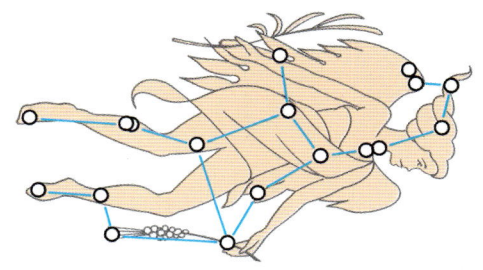

Virgo is the largest constellation in the **zodiac**. Virgo's brightest star is Spica with a magnitude of about 1. Not far from Spica is the Sombrero Galaxy. Looking like a hat with a wide brim, it is visible only through a telescope.

Many different stories explain the constellation Virgo. In one myth, Virgo is the goddess who holds the scales of justice, Libra. In another, Virgo is the goddess of corn, holding Spica, which means "head of grain". Yet another story tells of a young girl whose father has been killed. She cannot stop crying, so Zeus places her with her father, Boötes the herdsman, a constellation in the northern **celestial sphere**. See page 21 for more information.

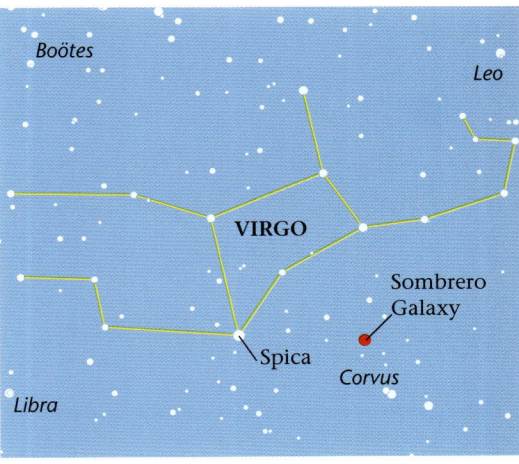

The Twenty Brightest Stars in the Sky

Rank	Star	Magnitude	Constellation
1	Sirius	−1.46	Canis Major
2	Canopus	−0.72	Carina
3	Alpha Centauri	−0.27	Centaurus
4	Arcturus	−0.04	Boötes
5	Vega	0.03	Lyra
6	Capella	0.08	Auriga
7	Rigel	0.12	Orion
8	Procyon	0.38	Canis Minor
9	Achernar	0.46	Eridanus
10	Betelgeuse	0.50	Orion
11	Hadar	0.61	Centaurus
12	Acrux	0.76	Crux
13	Altair	0.77	Aquila
14	Aldebaran	0.85	Taurus
15	Antares	0.96	Scorpius
16	Spica	0.98	Virgo
17	Pollux	1.14	Gemini
18	Fomalhaut	1.16	Piscis Austrinus
19	Deneb	1.25	Cygnus
20	Beta Crucis	1.25	Crux

The Sombrero Galaxy

Best Viewing Time

April to June
Where: 67°N–75°S

Constellations of the Northern and Southern Celestial Spheres

This section includes, in alphabetical order, many of the **constellations** that are not in the **zodiac**. Remember that the stars that will be visible to you depend on where you live and the time of year you are viewing them. Stars that circle the North Pole or South Pole, called circumpolar stars, can be seen year-round by people who live in that hemisphere. In the Northern Hemisphere, circumpolar constellations include Ursa Major, Cassiopeia and Draco. In the Southern Hemisphere, circumpolar constellations include Triangulum Australe (the Southern Triangle) and Octans.

Andromeda
(an-DRAHM-uh-dah)

Best Viewing Time

October to November
Where: 90°N–37°S

Andromeda lies near Cassiopeia (kas-see-oh-PEE-ah) and Cepheus (SEE-fee-us). It contains the Andromeda Galaxy, the nearest major **galaxy** to Earth. In Greek **myths**, Cassiopeia and Cepheus were rulers of a large country. Queen Cassiopeia boasted that both she and her daughter, Andromeda, were more beautiful than the sea nymphs. This angered the sea god Poseidon, who threatened to destroy their lands by sending a sea monster and floods.

King Cepheus was advised to sacrifice his daughter to the sea monster to save his land. Fortunately, the hero Perseus saw Andromeda chained to a rock and fell in love with her. He killed the sea monster and married Andromeda.

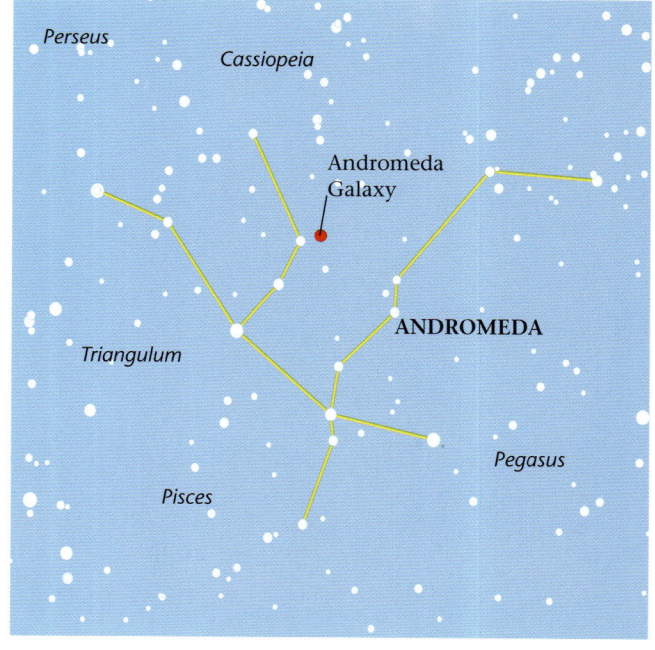

Aquila

(uh-KEEL-uh), the Eagle

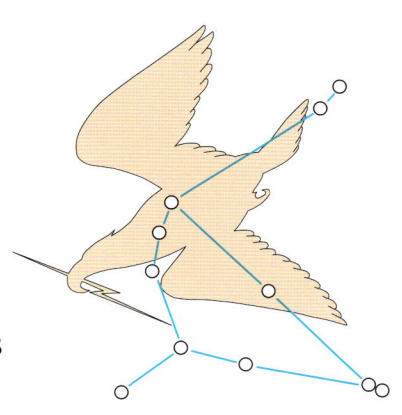

Aquila is a prominent constellation with the **Milky Way** band of stars running through it. Altair, the thirteenth brightest star, is on the Eagle's neck. Sixteen **light-years** away from Earth, Altair would shine nine times more brightly than the Sun if placed next to it. The constellation includes a number of **double stars** and **nebulae**. For at least 3,500 years, Aquila has been identified with a bird. It has been an eagle, a raven, a hawk and a vulture to various cultures. In Roman mythology, Aquila was the eagle sent to collect Ganymede, or Aquarius, who was chosen to be cupbearer to the gods.

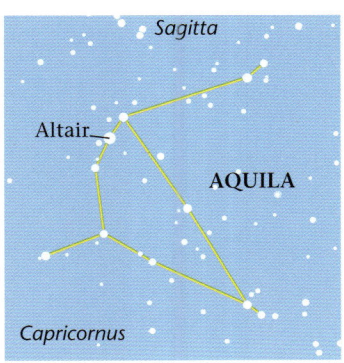

Best Viewing Time

July to August
Where: 78°N–71°S

Boötes

(boh-OH-teez), the Herdsman

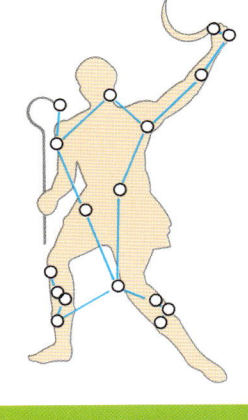

Arcturus (ark-TUR-us) is the brightest star in the constellation Boötes. Arcturus is Greek for "bear guard".

In Greek myths, Boötes represents Arcas, the son of Callisto. When Callisto was changed into a bear, Arcas did not recognize her as his mother and tried to slay her. Zeus prevented this tragedy by placing them both in the sky. As the bear driver, or herdsman, Boötes chases the Great Bear (Ursa Major) and the Lesser Bear (Ursa Minor) across the sky.

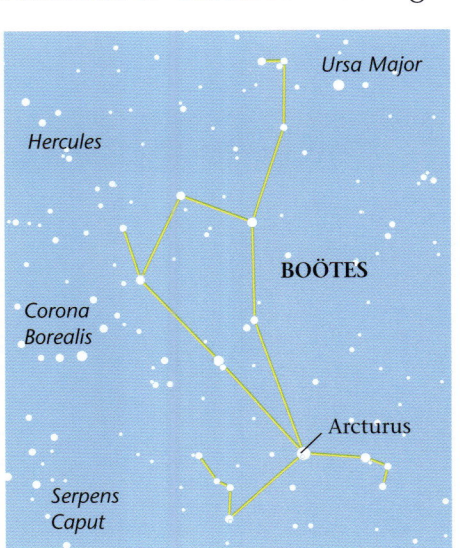

Best Viewing Time

May to June
Where: 90°N–35°S

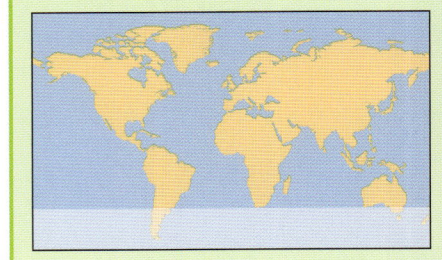

Canis Major

(KAY-nihs MAY-juhr), the Greater Dog

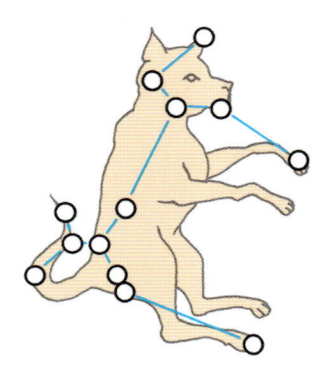

Canis Major contains the brightest star in the night sky, Sirius, which is also known as the Dog Star. Sirius is relatively close to Earth – only about 8.6 light years away – and is easily visible from most places on Earth.

Sirius is also a **double star**. Its companion is popularly called the Pup (Puppis). The **constellation** Canis Major represents one of Orion's dogs. It appears to be running after Orion, the Hunter, in the night sky.

Best Viewing Time

January to February
Where: 56°N–90°S

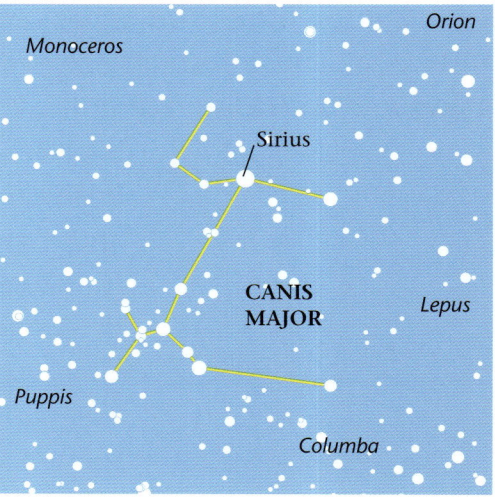

Canis Minor

(KAY-nihs MY-nuhr), the Lesser Dog

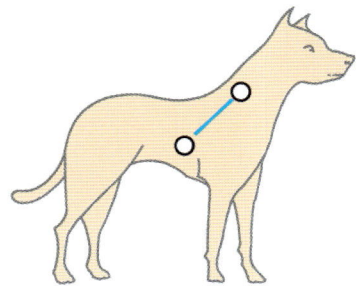

Canis Minor contains the eighth brightest star in the sky, Procyon (proh-SY-uhn), a name that means "before the dog". This constellation represents the smaller of Orion's two dogs. It appears near both Orion and his other dog, Canis Major.

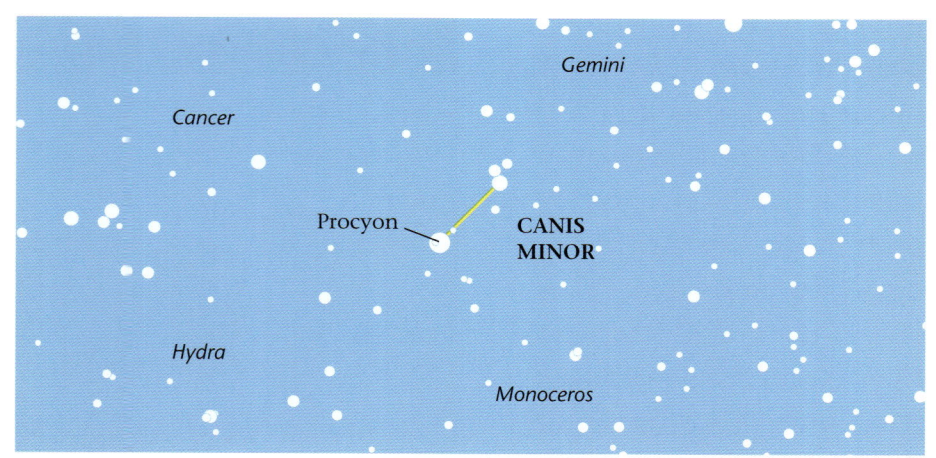

Best Viewing Time

February
Where: 89°N–77°S

Carina
(kuh-RY-nah), the Keel

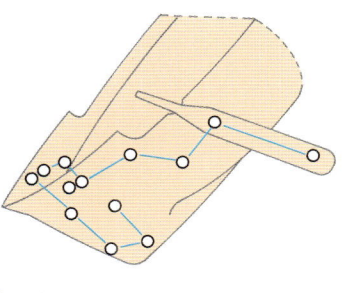

Best Viewing Time

January to April
Where: 14°N–90°S

Carina was once seen as part of a massive constellation called Argo Navis, a giant ship that carried Jason and the Argonauts in search of the Golden Fleece. Later, Argo Navis was split into three separate constellations. Carina is named after the keel, the bottom of the ship. Like the keels of ancient ships, the constellation has a U-shape.

Carina contains Canopus, the second brightest star in the sky. It also contains Eta Carinae, a star with a mass 100 times that of our Sun. Scientists believe that this star will probably explode as a **supernova** eventually. Such an explosion occurs with some massive stars when they grow old.

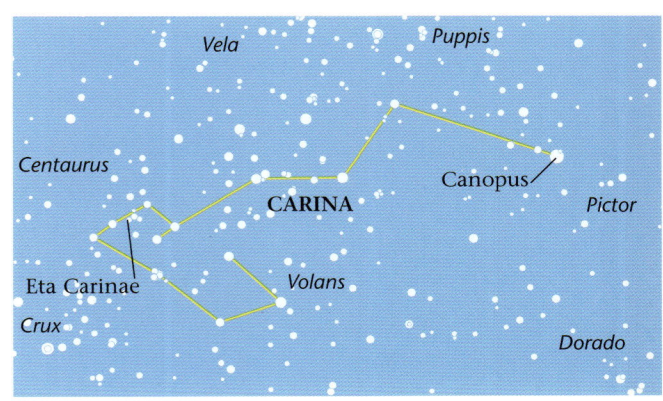

Centaurus
(sen-TAWR-uhs), the Centaur

Centaurus contains Alpha Centauri (or Rigil Kentaurus), the third brightest star in the night sky. Composed of several stars, Alpha Centauri contains the star that is closest to the Sun.

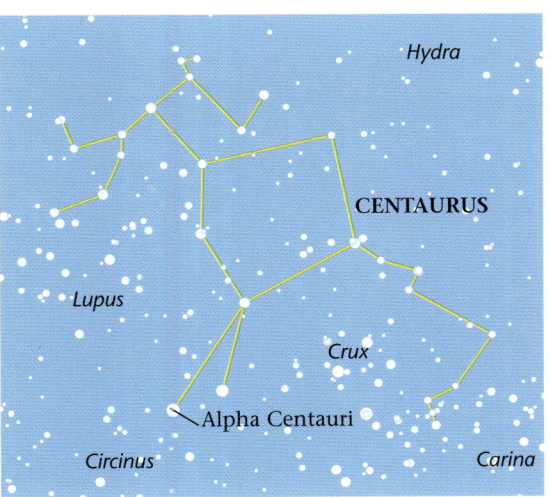

Centaurus is meant to represent the famous centaur Chiron (SHEER-on), the wisest of all creatures. The son of the god Saturn, Chiron taught Jason and other Greek heroes many important skills, including how to navigate by the stars.

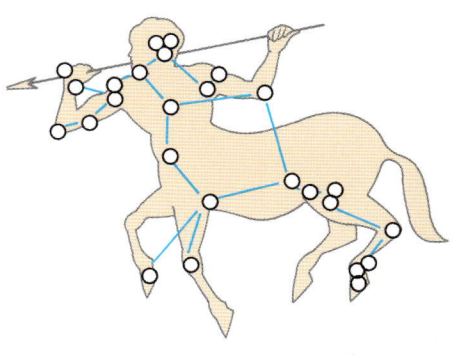

Best Viewing Time

April to June
Where: 25°N–90°S

23

Cepheus

(SEE-fee-us), the Monarch

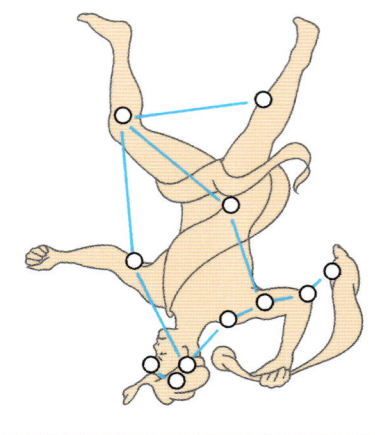

Cepheus is a large, northern **constellation**. The constellation looks a little like a lopsided square wearing a tall, pointed cap. This constellation gave its name to the cepheids, a group of stars that vary in brightness in a very regular, repeating pattern. The first cepheid to be identified was in Cepheus. In Greek mythology, King Cepheus was Andromeda's father. He ruled the northern skies along with Cassiopeia.

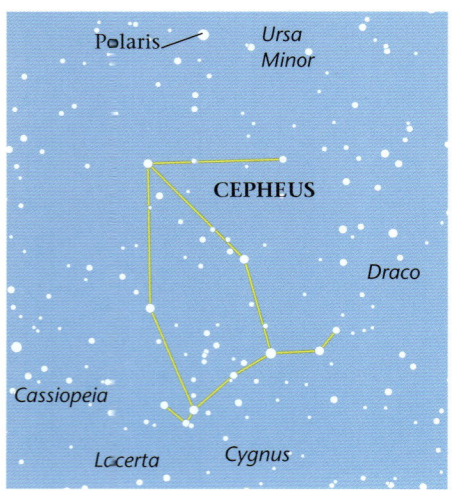

Best Viewing Time

September to October
Where: 90°N–1°S

Corona Australis

(kohr-OH-nah aws-TRAL-ihs), the Southern Crown

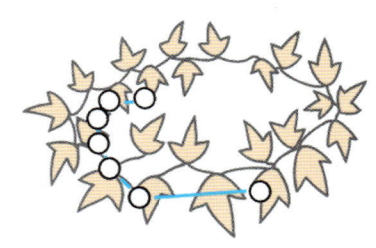

Corona Australis contains an arc of stars. The brightest star in the arc has a magnitude of about 4. The ancient Greeks thought of this constellation as a wreath or crown lying at the front feet of Sagittarius, the archer. The Northern Hemisphere also has a crown-shaped constellation – Corona Borealis (BOR-ee-AHL-is), the Northern Crown.

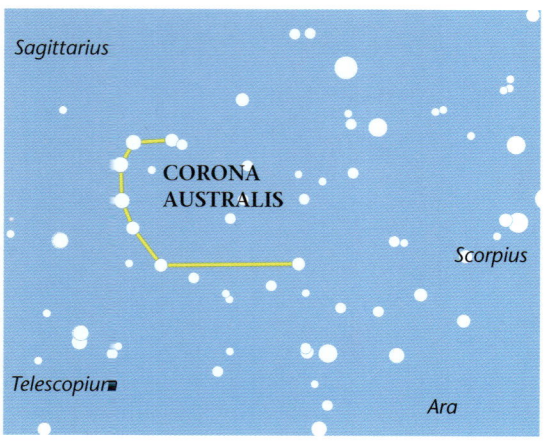

Best Viewing Time

July to August
Where: 44°N–90°S

Crux

(kruhks), the Southern Cross

Crux points to the south **celestial** pole and shows where south is on the horizon. Almost completely surrounded by Centaurus, it was considered part of that constellation until late in the sixteenth century. European sailors considered Crux so important that it was included in the flags of Australia, New Zealand, Brazil, Samoa and Papua New Guinea.

Crux is a cross-shaped constellation formed by four stars, including Acrux, the twelfth brightest star. Crux contains a famous **nebula** called the Coalsack. This dark cloud of dust and gas is silhouetted against a background of more distant stars.

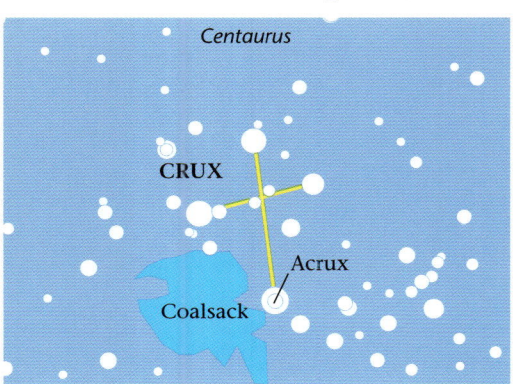

The main stars in Crux

Best Viewing Time

April to May
Where: 25°N–90°S

Cygnus

(SIHG-nuhs), the Swan

Cygnus lies near Cepheus. Its brightest star, called Deneb, pours out more light in one night than our Sun does in 100 years. Cygnus is Greek for "swan", and this cross-shaped constellation has been seen as a bird for thousands of years. Deneb, located on the tail of the bird, means "tail". Cygnus X-1, which may be a **black hole**, is also part of the Swan.

Best Viewing Time

August to September
Where: 90°N–28°S

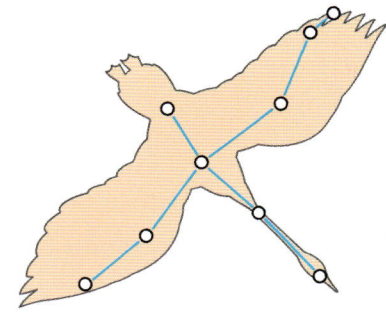

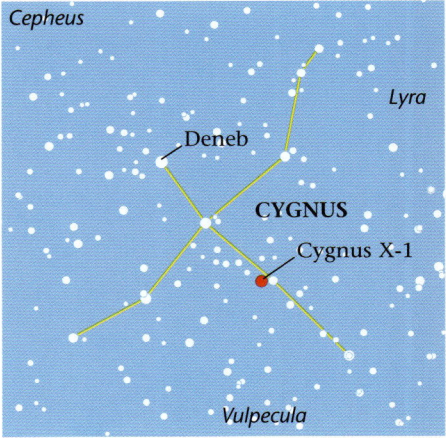

25

Dorado

(doh-RAH-doh), the Goldfish

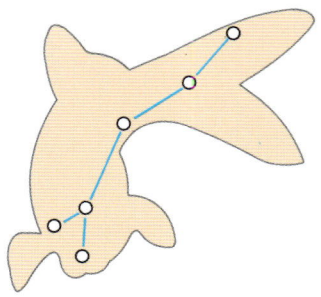

Dorado contains much of the Large Magellanic Cloud, a small **galaxy** close to the Milky Way. When a **supernova** exploded in this galaxy in 1987, astronomers observed it with powerful scientific instruments. As a result, they gained new knowledge about the life cycle of stars. This constellation represents a gold-coloured tropical sea fish called the dorado, also known as the dolphinfish.

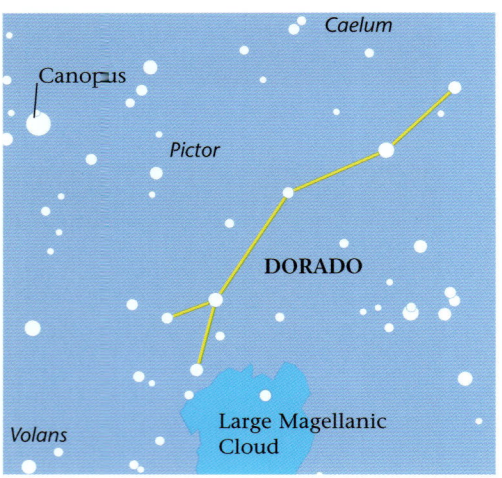

Best Viewing Time

December to January
Where: 20°N–90°S

Draco

(DRAY-koh), the Dragon

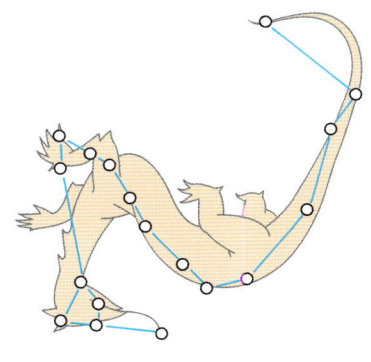

Draco is a long and winding **constellation**. Its tail almost wraps around Ursa Minor, but the easiest way to find it is to look for the four brighter stars that make up its head. The Cat's Eye Nebula can be found in this constellation.

In Greek legend, one of Hercules's twelve labours was to steal three golden apples from the tree that the goddess of Earth, Gaia, had given to Hera, queen of the Greek gods. Draco had been assigned to guard the tree. Hercules, however, approached Draco from the sky and killed the dragon with an arrow.

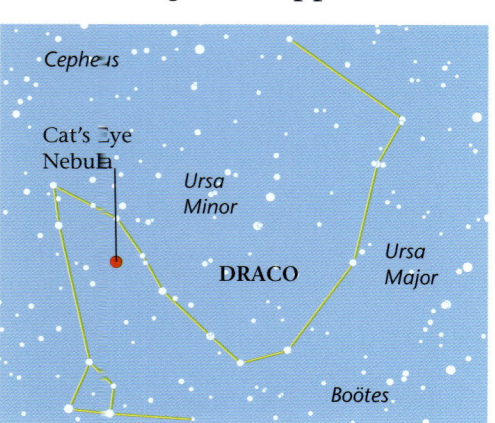

Best Viewing Time

March to September
Where: 90°N–4°S

Eridanus

(ih-RID-a-nuhs), the River

Eridanus is a long constellation. It runs from Rigel, the bright star in Orion, to Achernar, the brightest star in Eridanus, located near the south **celestial** pole. Eridanus is believed to contain a star, Epsilon Eridani, with an orbiting planet. Thousands of years ago, this constellation was seen as the Nile or Euphrates River.

Best Viewing Time

November to January
Where: 32°N–89°S

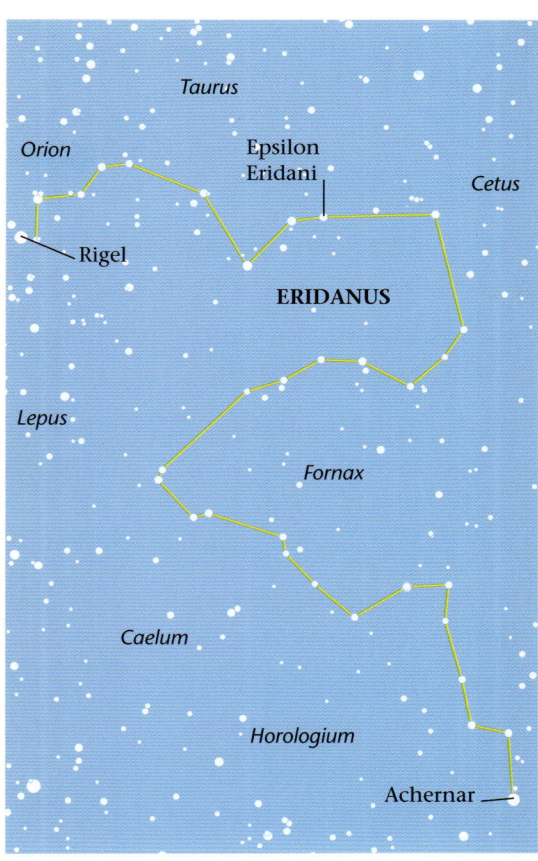

Hercules

(HER-ku-leez)

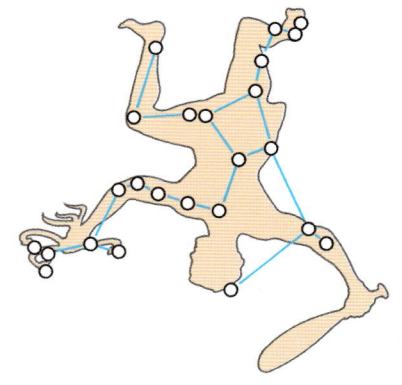

The constellation Hercules can be found between Boötes and Lyra. Four bright stars, known as the "Keystone of Hercules", make up the Greek hero's kneeling body.

Hercules was a strong and courageous fighter in Greek myths. Many of the twelve labours that he was given to complete involved fighting fierce creatures. Some of the creatures, such as Leo, Hydra and Taurus, are represented in other constellations.

Best Viewing Time

June to August
Where: 90°N–38°S

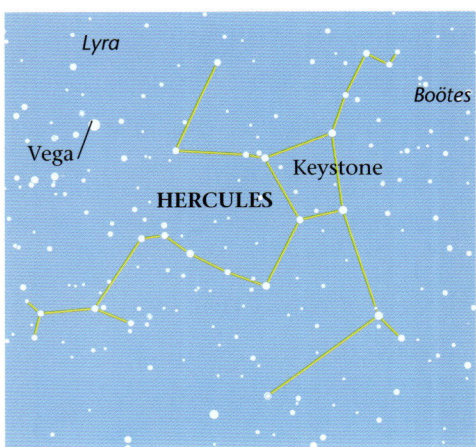

27

Hydra

(HY-crah), the Sea Serpent

Best Viewing Time

February to June
Where: 54°N–83°S

Hydra is the largest **constellation**. It is made up of a broken line of faint stars not far from the **ecliptic**, with its head near Cancer and its tail near Libra. The brightest star is called Alphard, which means "the solitary one".

Hydra was a water monster with many snake-like heads. A single glimpse of Hydra caused people to die of fright. Hercules tried cutting off Hydra's heads, but three new ones grew in the place of each one he cut off. Eventually, he destroyed the monster with fire.

Hydrus

(HY-druhs), the Water Snake

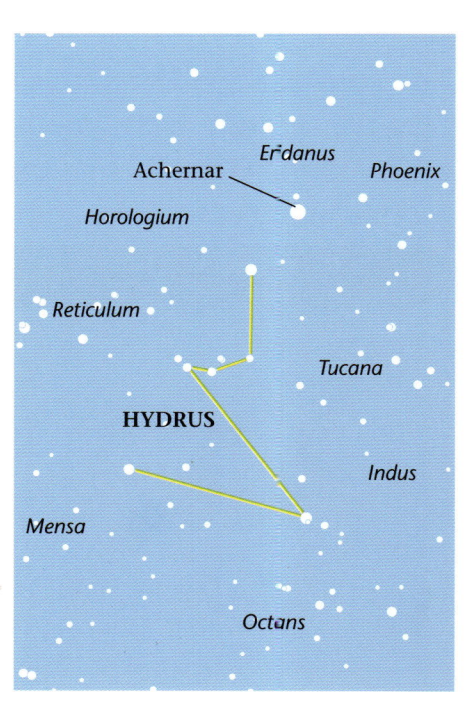

Best Viewing Time

October to December
Where: 8°N–90°S

This **constellation** lies between the bright star Achernar and the south celestial pole. In the late sixteenth century, Dutch navigators named it after a small water snake. Hydrus should not be confused with Hydra, which is seen in the Northern Hemisphere.

Lepus
(LEH-puhs), the Hare

Lepus lies near Orion, between Orion's bright star Rigel and the bright star Sirius. Lepus's brightest star, Arneb, is magnitude 2.6.

Hares and rabbits damaged the crops of the ancient Greeks, so the Greeks were happy to see a hare-shaped constellation at the feet of the hunter Orion. He and his dog, Canis Major, hunt the hare as they move across the night sky.

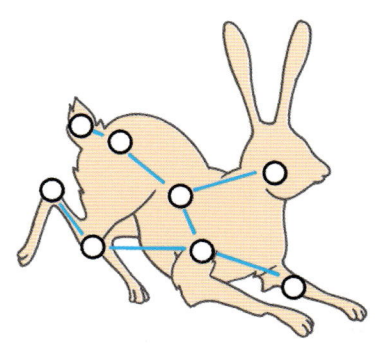

Best Viewing Time
January
Where: 62°N–90°S

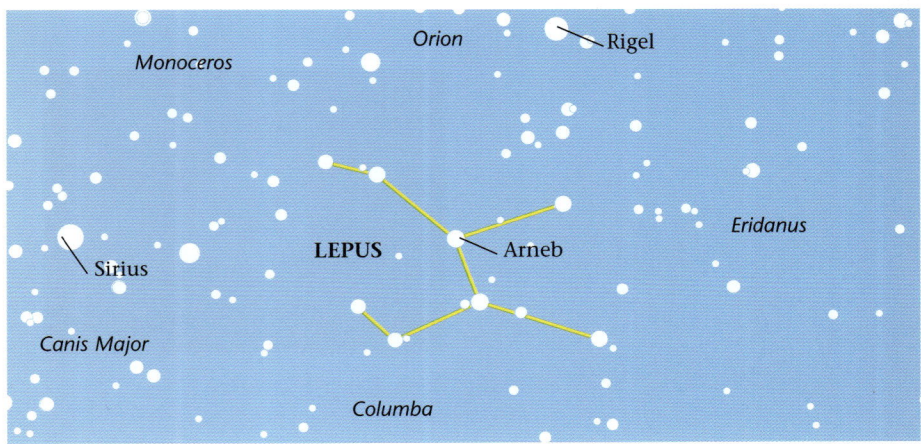

Lupus
(LOO-puhs), the Wolf

Lupus, the Wolf, lies in the Milky Way band of stars. Its brightest star is Alpha Lupi, which has a magnitude of 2.3. Greeks and Romans thought of it as a wolf held on a pole by Centaurus, the centaur. However, they had no myths about Lupus.

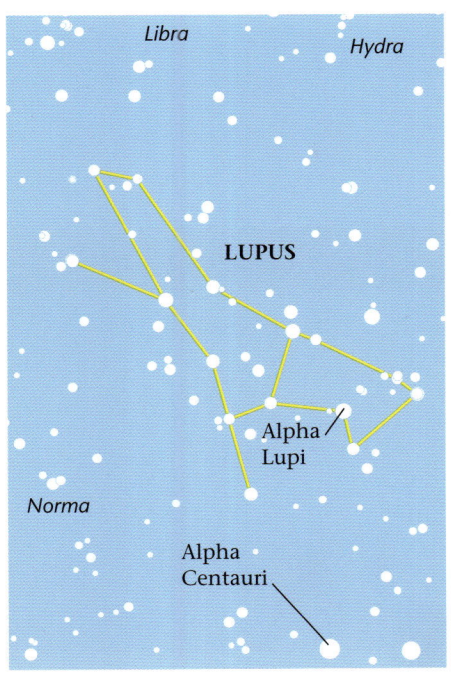

Best Viewing Time
May to June
Where: 34°N–90°S

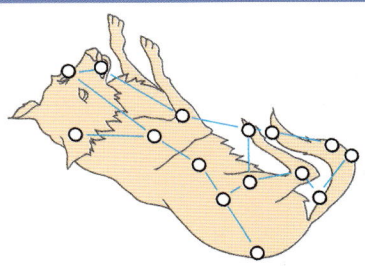

Lyra

(LIH-rah), the Lyre

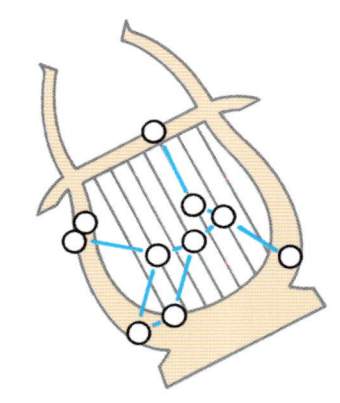

Lyra contains Vega, the fifth brightest star, with a magnitude of 0.03 Lyra also contains a quadruple star and the Ring Nebula a glowing ring of gas given off by a dying star.

A lyre is a stringed instrument that looks like a small harp. In one Greek myth, the lyre belonged to the great musician Orpheus. After his death, the lyre continued to play sad songs endlessly until the gods placed it high in the sky.

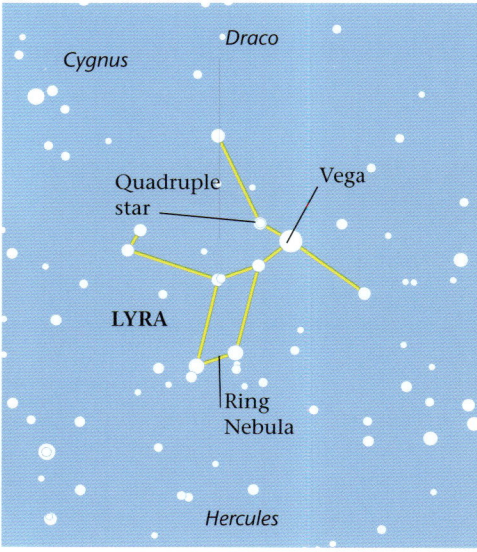

Best Viewing Time

July to August
Where: 90°N–42°S

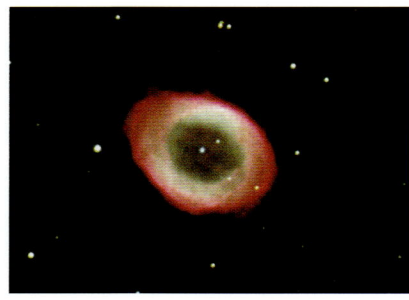

The Ring Nebula

Mensa

(MEN-sah), the Table

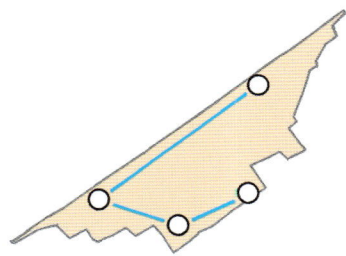

Mensa is not a bright **constellation**, but it does contain part of the Large Magellanic Cloud, also found in the constellation Dorado. In the 1700s, the astronomer Nicolas Louis de Lacaille named the constellation Mons Mensae, or Table Mountain, from a site in Cape Town, South Africa, where he had observed the stars for many years. Today, the constellation is simply called Mensa, or the Table.

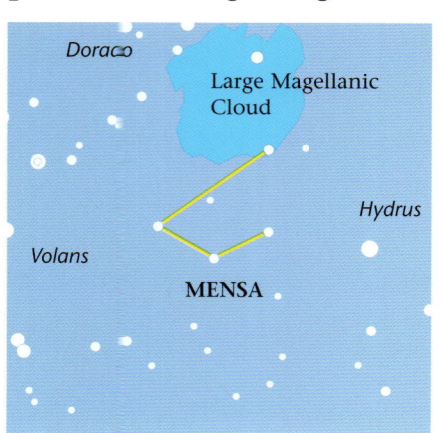

Best Viewing Time

December to February
Where: 5°N–90°S

Octans

(AHK-tahnz), the Octant

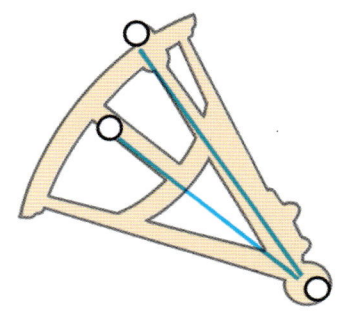

This constellation contains Sigma Octantis, the nearest star to the south **celestial** pole that can be seen without a telescope. Sigma Octantis is quite faint. Therefore, it is not used for navigation, as Polaris, the North Star, is.

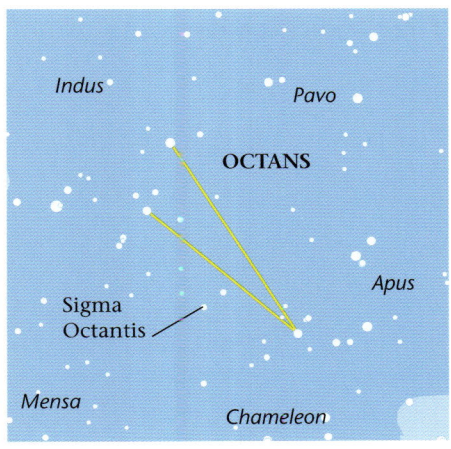

An octant is a triangular instrument used to navigate the seas. It was invented around 1730. Astronomer Nicolas Louis de Lacaille introduced this constellation soon after the invention of the octant, to honour the important scientific instrument.

Best Viewing Time

October
Where: 0°N–90°S

Ophiuchus

(AH-fee-YOO-kuhs), the Serpent Bearer

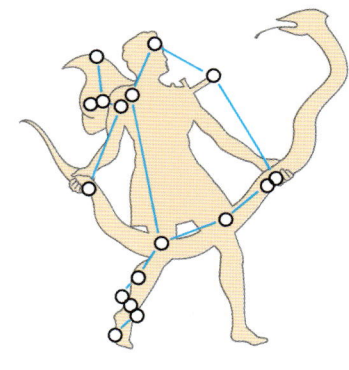

Ophiuchus sprawls across the sky between Hercules and Scorpius. Many astronomers consider Ophiuchus to be part of the zodiac because it lies along the **ecliptic**. Ophiuchus

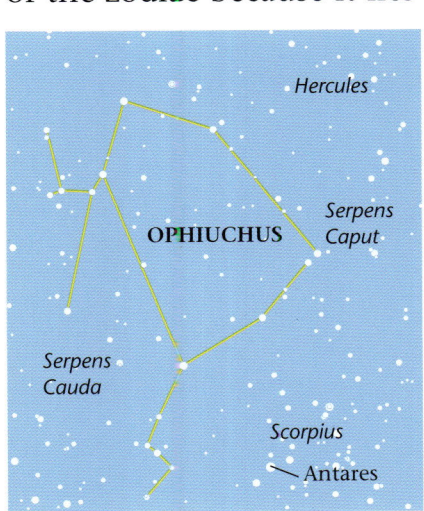

divides another constellation, Serpens, into two: Serpens Caput (the Serpent's Head) and Serpens Cauda (the Serpent's Tail). The Greeks believed that the constellation Ophiuchus honoured Asclepius, the son of the god Apollo. A legendary hero, Asclepius is shown holding the snake, Serpens, a symbol of healing.

Best Viewing Time

June to July
Where: 59°N–75°S

Orion

(oh-RY-uhn), the Hunter

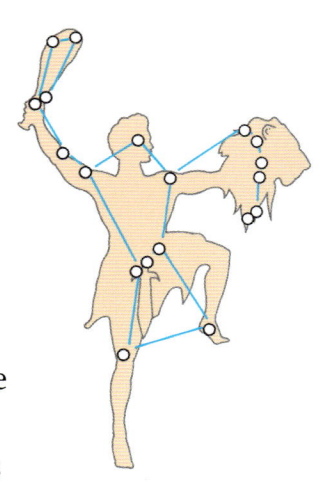

Orion is the brightest of all the ancient **constellations**. The stars Betelgeuse, Bellatrix, Rigel and Saiph mark the figure of the hunter. Betelgeuse has a diameter 800 times greater than the Sun's. Orion's belt is formed by three other stars, close together in a line. The hunter's sword, hanging down from the belt, contains the Orion Nebula, which is visible to the unaided eye on a clear night.

In Greek mythology, Orion died after Scorpius stung him. Artemis, the goddess of hunting, was so sad that she put Orion in the sky as a constellation. Earlier civilizations, such as Arabia, also recognized the constellation, often seeing it as a man or a giant.

The Orion Nebula

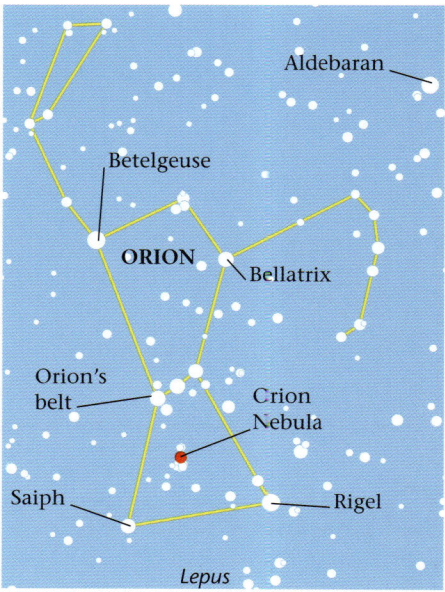

Best Viewing Time

December to January
Where: 79°N–67°S

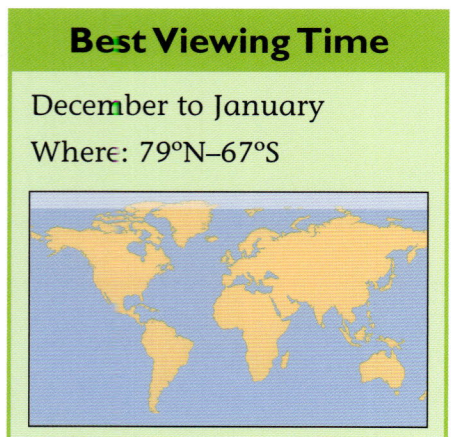

Pegasus

(PEGH-ah-suhs), the Winged Horse

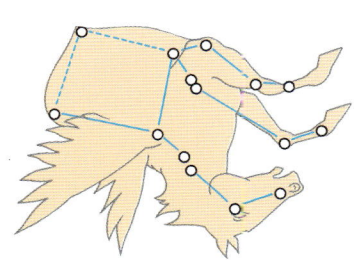

This is a large **constellation** north of Aquarius and Pisces that represents the front half of a winged horse. In Greek mythology, the horse sprang from the head of Medusa after Perseus beheaded her.

Best Viewing Time

September to October
Where: 90°N–53°S

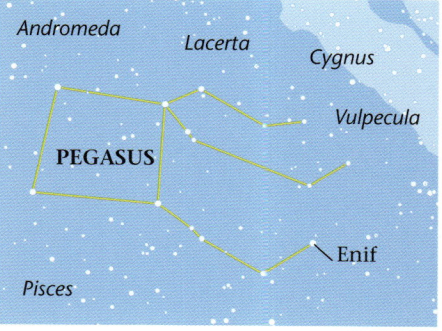

Perseus

(PER-see-uhs), the Hero

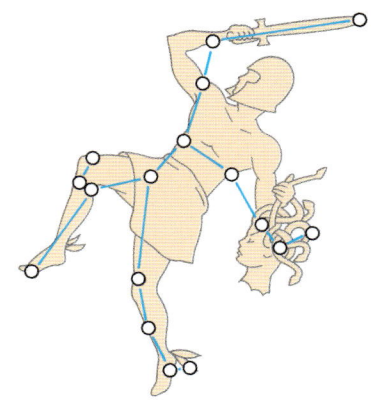

Perseus is near Cassiopeia and Andromeda. The Perseid meteor shower in August, a spectacular display, seems to come from this constellation. Perseus's brightest star is Mirfak. Its second brightest star, Algol, varies in brightness. This **variable star** represents the eye of Medusa. According to Greek legend, her evil glance turned a person to stone. Perseus killed Medusa. He was also the hero who rescued Andromeda.

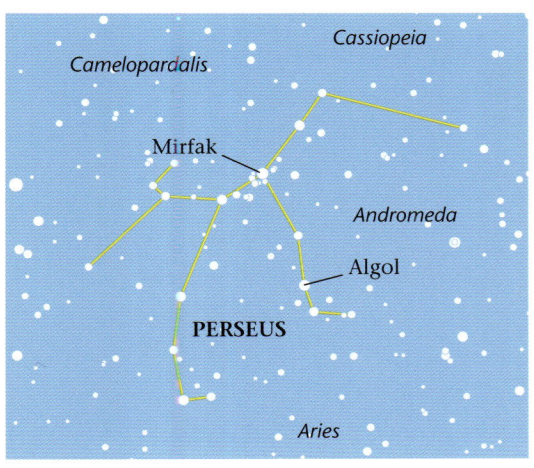

Best Viewing Time

November to December
Where: 90°N–31°S

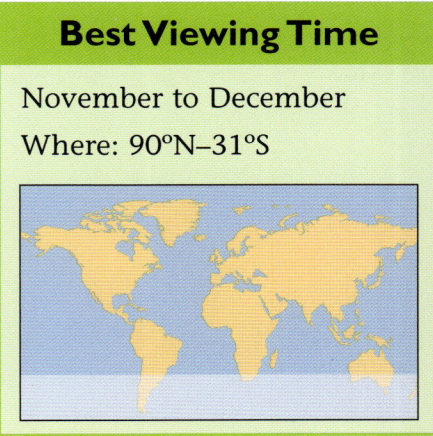

Piscis Austrinus

(PY-sis aws-TREE-nuhs), the Southern Fish

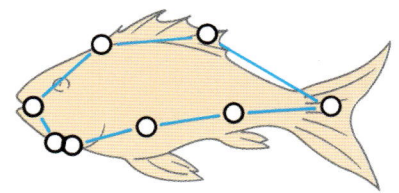

This fish appears near Aquarius, seeming to drink from the water carrier's jar. One of its stars, Fomalhaut, with a magnitude of about 1.2, is among the 20 brightest stars. The ancient Greeks thought of this fish as the parent of the two fish in Pisces.

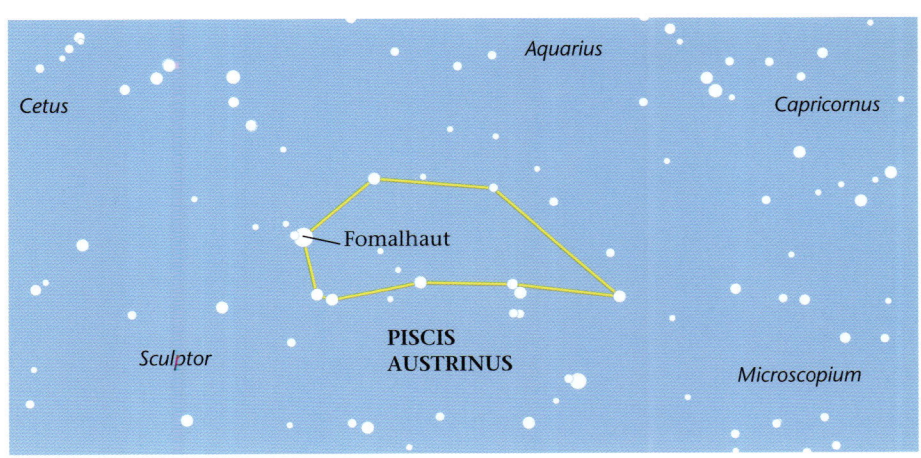

Best Viewing Time

September to October
Where: 53°N–90°S

Puppis

(PUHP-pihs), the Stern

Puppis lies in the Milky Way near Canis Major. Ancient Greeks thought of it as the stern of the *Argo*, the ship that took Jason and his Argonauts on their quest for the Golden Fleece.

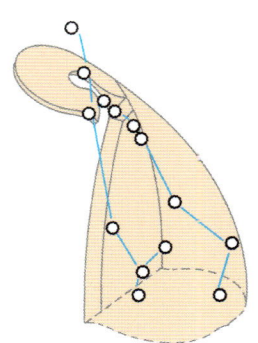

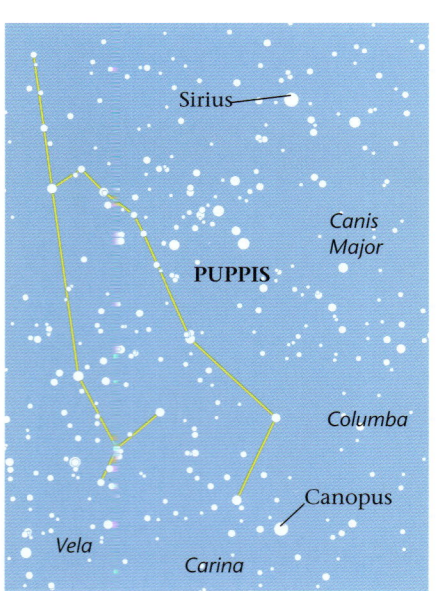

Best Viewing Time

January to February
Where: 39°N–90°S

Jason and the Argonauts

Jason was a Greek prince whose uncle Pelics cheated him out of his kingdom. When Jason tried to reclaim his throne, his uncle insisted that Jason must first bring him the Golden Fleece. This fleece, the hide of Mercury's magical ram (see Aries, page 12), had healing powers. Jason obtained the fleece with the help of the Argonauts, his brave crew on the *Argo*.

Serpens

(SER-pehnz), the Serpent

This constellation is unique in that it is split in two. Ophiuchus, the Serpent Bearer, holds the serpent's head in one hand and its tail in the other. The serpent is the symbol for poison (venom) that can kill or cure, and was one of the 48 listed by Ptolemy.

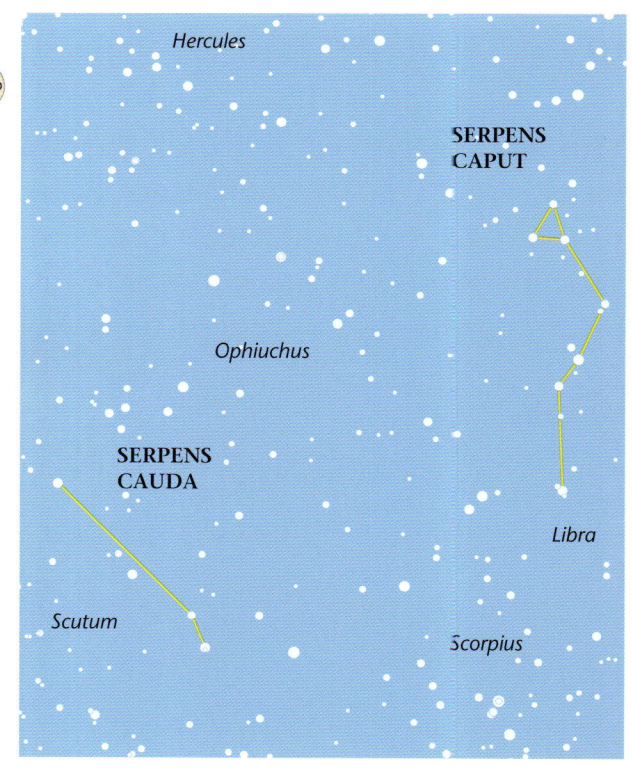

Best Viewing Time

June to August
Where: 74°N–64°S

Triangulum Australe

(try-AN-goo-luhm aws-TRAHL), the Southern Triangle

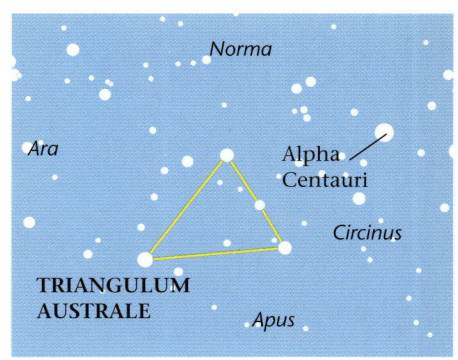

Triangulum Australe lies near Alpha Centauri (Rigil Kentaurus), the third brightest star. The Southern Triangle, as this constellation is known, lies mostly in the Milky Way. It was identified by the German astronomer Johann Bayer in 1603. It has a counterpart in the northern **celestial** hemisphere – another triangle-shaped constellation that is called Triangulum.

Triangulum Australe

Best Viewing Time

June to July
Where: 19°N–90°S

Tucana

(too-KAH-nah), the Toucan

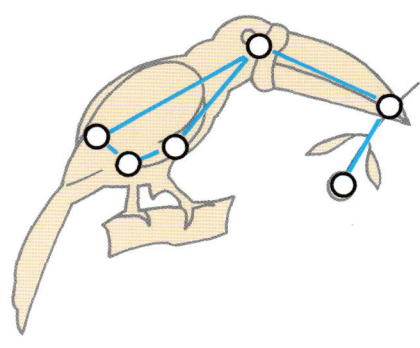

Near the South Pole, Tucana contains the Small Magellanic Cloud, a small **galaxy** that is near the Milky Way. The constellation was named by Dutch navigators in the late sixteenth century and appeared in Johann Bayer's star chart of 1603. At that time, Europeans had just become aware of the colourful, big-billed South American birds.

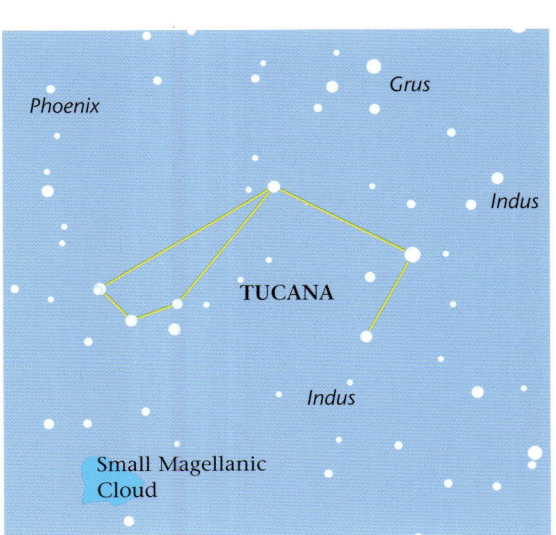

Best Viewing Time

September to November
Where: 14°N–90°S

Ursa Major

(ER-sah MAY-jihr), the Great Bear

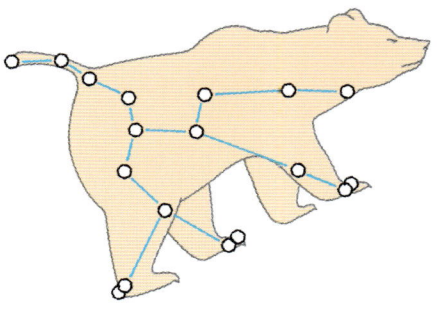

Ursa Major is one of the best-known constellations in the Northern Hemisphere. It contains the Big Dipper, or the Plough, an **asterism** of seven bright stars that can be seen as a dipper, or pot, with a handle. The second star from the end of the dipper's handle, Mizar, seems to be a **double star** with Alcor. However, they only appear to be "close" because they are both in the same line of sight. Astronomers now know that Alcor is itself a binary star – two stars bound together by gravity.

Several cultures saw this constellation as a big bear in the sky. Legends from other places described this constellation as a wagon or as hunters chasing a bear or skunk.

In Greek mythology, Hera, the queen of the gods, became jealous of the lovely Callisto and changed her into a bear. Zeus put the bear Callisto into the sky as Ursa Major.

Best Viewing Time

February to May
Where: 90°N–16°S

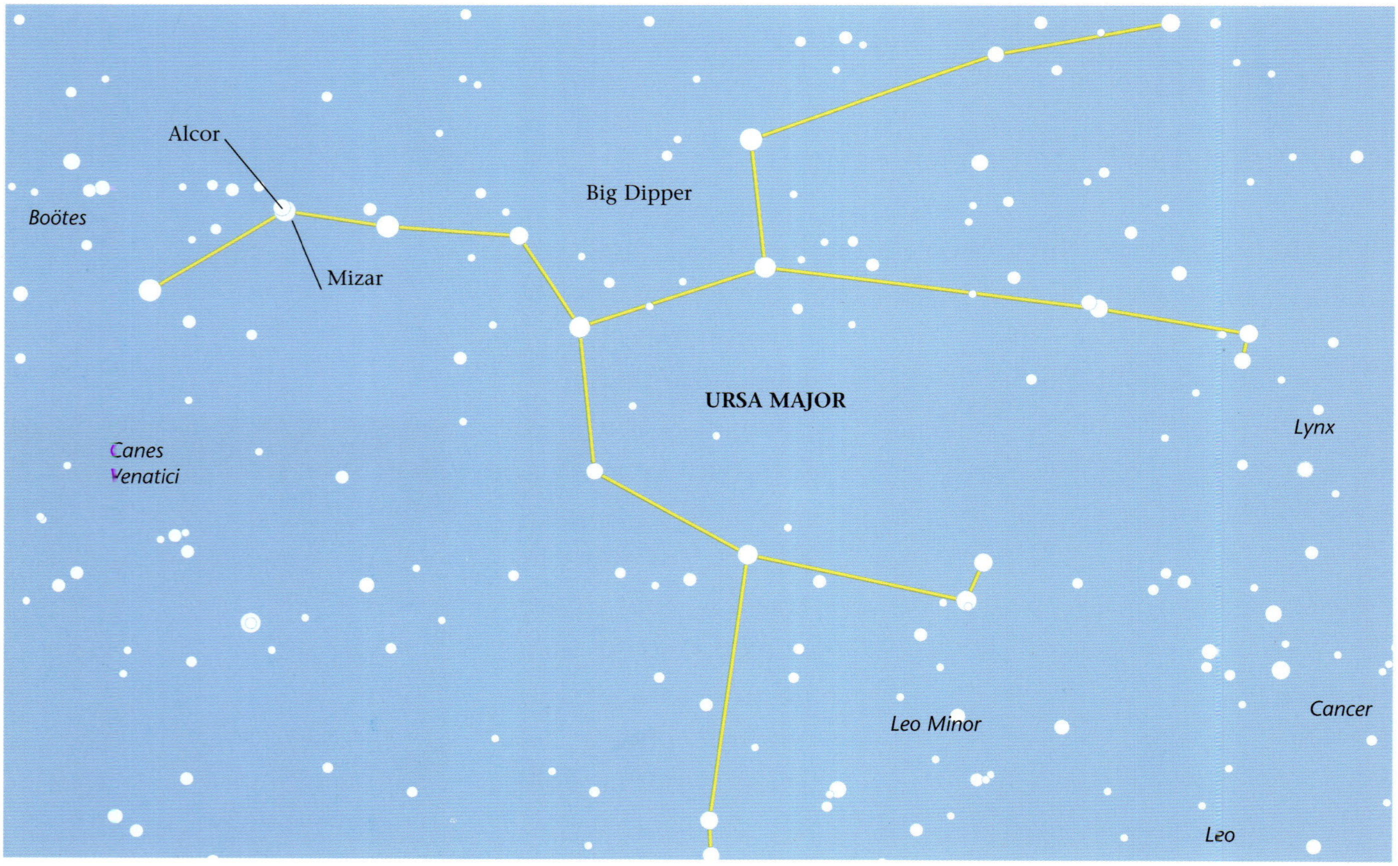

Ursa Minor
(ER-sah MY-nihr), the Lesser Bear

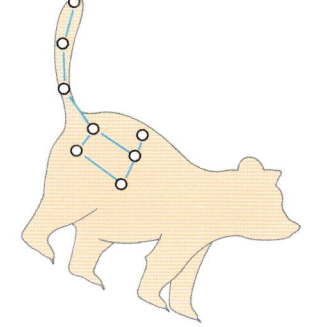

Ursa Minor contains the Little Dipper, seven stars that can be seen as a dipper with a handle. The constellation's brightest star, Polaris, or the North Star, heads a little closer to the north **celestial** pole each year. (It will be closest in 2095.) The star Kochab is in the bowl of the Little Dipper. About the same brightness as Polaris, it is yellower than the North Star and often easier to spot.

In Greek mythology Zeus turned Callisto's son, Arcas, into a small bear and put him into the sky as Ursa Minor, to keep his mother company.

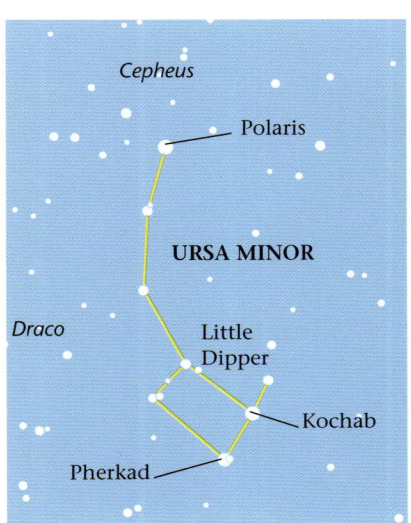

The North Star

The North Star, or Polaris, is almost directly over the North Pole. As Earth revolves, Polaris doesn't appear to move. It is a constant in a changing sky and helps sailors to navigate. Polaris is also called the Pole Star and the Navigator's Star.

Best Viewing Time

May to June
Where: 90°N–0°S

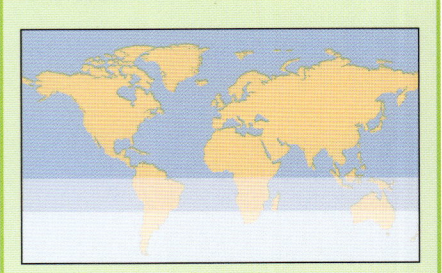

Vela
(VAY-lah), the Sails

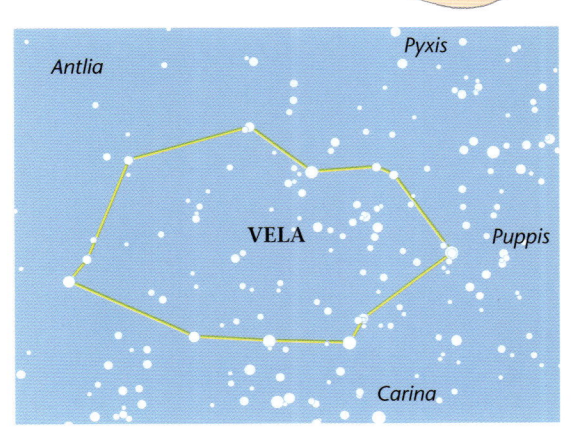

This constellation represents the sails of the *Argo*, the ship of Jason and the Argonauts. It lies near the other two parts of the ship – Carina, the keel, and Puppis, the stern.

Best Viewing Time

February to April
Where: 32°N–90°S

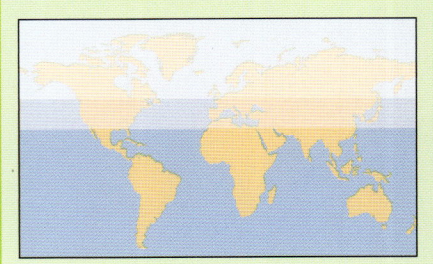

The Eighty-Eight Constellations

The International Astronomical Union (IAU) publishes the sky atlas most often used today, recognizing eighty-eight official constellations.

Constellation	Meaning	Constellation	Meaning
Andromeda	Andromeda	Lacerta	Lizard
Antlia	Pump	Leo	Lion
Apus	Bird of Paradise	Leo Minor	Lesser Lion
Aquarius	Water Carrier	Lepus	Hare
Aquila	Eagle	Libra	Scales
Ara	Altar	Lupus	Wolf
Aries	Ram	Lynx	Lynx
Auriga	Charioteer	Lyra	Lyre
Boötes	Herdsman	Mensa	Table
Caelum	Chisel	Microscopium	Microscope
Camelopardalis	Giraffe	Monoceros	Unicorn
Cancer	Crab	Musca	Fly
Canes Venatici	Hunting Dogs	Norma	Square
Canis Major	Greater Dog	Octans	Octant
Canis Minor	Lesser Dog	Ophiuchus	Serpent Bearer
Capricornus	Sea Goat	Orion	Orion
Carina	Keel	Pavo	Peacock
Cassiopeia	Cassiopeia	Pegasus	Pegasus
Centaurus	Centaur	Perseus	Perseus
Cepheus	Monarch	Phoenix	Phoenix
Cetus	Whale	Pictor	Easel
Chamaeleon	Chameleon	Pisces	Fish
Circinus	Drawing Compass	Piscis Austrinus	Southern Fish
Columba	Dove	Puppis	Stern (of a ship)
Coma Berenices	Berenice's Hair	Pyxis	Compass
Corona Australis	Southern Crown	Reticulum	Reticle (or Net)
Corona Borealis	Northern Crown	Sagitta	Arrow
Corvus	Raven	Sagittarius	Archer
Crater	Cup	Scorpius	Scorpion
Crux	Southern Cross	Sculptor	Sculptor
Cygnus	Swan	Scutum	Shield
Delphinus	Dolphin	Serpens	Serpent
Dorado	Goldfish	Sextans	Sextant
Draco	Dragon	Taurus	Bull
Equuleus	Little Horse	Telescopium	Telescope
Eridanus	River	Triangulum	Triangle
Fornax	Furnace	Triangulum Australe	Southern Triangle
Gemini	Twins	Tucana	Toucan
Grus	Crane	Ursa Major	Great Bear
Hercules	Hercules	Ursa Minor	Lesser Bear
Horologium	Clock	Vela	Sails
Hydra	Sea Serpent	Virgo	Virgin
Hydrus	Water Snake	Volans	Flying Fish
Indus	Indian	Vulpecula	Fox

Glossary

asterisms	small groups of stars that form a recognizable pattern or shape
astronomers	scientists who study the universe
black hole	an object with gravity so strong that even light cannot escape from it
celestial	having to do with the sky
celestial sphere	an imaginary sphere whose centre is the Earth, used by astronomers to map celestial objects
constellations	patterns of stars that can be imagined as figures or pictures
double star	two stars that appear close to one another in the sky. Some double stars are physically separate. Others, called binary stars, orbit around a common point.
ecliptic	the path followed by the Sun in the sky
equator	an imaginary circle around Earth (or another celestial body), halfway between the North Pole and South Pole
galaxies	huge collections of stars, gas, dust and other celestial bodies, all held together by gravity
light-years	units of measurement based on the distance light travels in a year
magnitude	a measure of the brightness of stars
Milky Way	the galaxy containing our Sun and solar system and hundreds of billions of stars; also the band of densely packed stars close to the centre of the galaxy
myths	stories that try to interpret some aspect of the world around us, such as a natural event
nebula	a huge cloud of gas and dust in space (pl: nebulae)
planisphere	a circular star map that can be turned to show which stars are in the sky at a chosen date and time
supernova	the explosion of a very large star at the end of its life
variable star	a star that varies in brightness over time
zodiac	a band of twelve constellations along the ecliptic

Constellations Index

Constellations of the Zodiac

Aquarius, the Water Carrier 12
Aries, the Ram 12
Cancer, the Crab 13
Capricornus, the Sea Goat 14
Gemini, the Twins 14
Leo, the Lion 15
Libra, the Scales 16
Pisces, the Fish 16
Sagittarius, the Archer 17
Scorpius, the Scorpion 18
Taurus, the Bull 18
Virgo, the Virgin 19

Constellations of the Northern and Southern Celestial Spheres

Andromeda 20
Aquila, the Eagle 21
Boötes, the Herdsman 21
Canis Major, the Greater Dog 22
Canis Minor, the Lesser Dog 22
Carina, the Keel 23
Centaurus, the Centaur 23
Cepheus 24
Corona Australis, the Southern Crown 24
Crux, the Southern Cross 25
Cygnus, the Swan 25
Dorado, the Goldfish 26
Draco, the Dragon 26
Eridanus, the River 27
Hercules 27
Hydra, the Sea Serpent 28
Hydrus, the Water Snake 28
Lepus, the Hare 29
Lupus, the Wolf 29
Lyra, the Lyre 30
Mensa, the Table 30
Octans, the Octant 31
Ophiuchus, the Serpent Bearer 31
Orion, the Hunter 32
Pegasus, the Winged Horse 32
Perseus, the Hero 33
Piscis Austrinus, the Southern Fish 33
Puppis, the Stern 34
Serpens, the Serpent 34
Triangulum Australe, the Southern Triangle 35
Tucana, the Toucan 35
Ursa Major, the Great Bear 36
Ursa Minor, the Lesser Bear 37
Vela, the Sails 37